NOW YOU KNOW

VOLUME 4

ALSO BY DOUG LENNOX

Now You Know
ISBN 1-55002-461-2 • $19.99, £10.99

Now You Know More
ISBN -1-55002-530-9 • $19.99, £10.99

Now You Know Almost Everything
ISBN 1-55002-575-9 •$19.99, £10.99

NOW YOU KNOW VOLUME 4

The Book of Answers

Doug Lennox

THE DUNDURN GROUP
TORONTO

Editor: Michael Carroll
Illustrations: Julia Bell
Design: Jennifer Scott
Printer: Transcontinental

Library and Archives Canada Cataloguing in Publication

Lennox, Doug
    Now you know : the book of answers / Doug Lennox.

Vol. 2 has title: Now you know more : the book of answers; v. 3 has
    title: Now you know almost everything.
ISBN 1-55002-461-2 (v. 1).--ISBN 1-55002-530-9 (v. 2)
ISBN 1-55002-575-9 (v. 3).--ISBN 1-55002-648-8 (v. 4)

1. Questions and answers. 2. Curiosities and wonders. I. Title. II. Title: Now you know more. III. Title: Now you know almost everything.

AG195.L45 2003   031.02   C2003-903531-X

1   2   3   4   5   10   08   07   06   06

 Conseil des Arts
du Canada
Canada Council
for the Arts
Canada

ONTARIO ARTS COUNCIL
CONSEIL DES ARTS DE L'ONTARIO

We acknowledge the support of the **Canada Council for the Arts** and the **Ontario Arts Council** for our publishing program. We also acknowledge the financial support of the **Government of Canada** through the **Book Publishing Industry Development Program** and **The Association for the Export of Canadian Books**, and the **Government of Ontario** through the **Ontario Book Publishers Tax Credit** program, and the **Ontario Media Development Corporation**.

Printed and bound in Canada.

www.dundurn.com

Dundurn Press
3 Church Street, Suite 500
Toronto, Ontario, Canada
M5E 1M2

Gazelle Book Services Limited
White Cross Mills
High Town, Lancaster, England
LA1 4XS

Dundurn Press
2250 Military Road
Tonawanda, NY
U.S.A. 14150

This book is dedicated to my aunt, Annie Lennox.

Among adults, there is no such thing as the truth,
only someone's idea of the truth. Truth is the exclusive
dominion of children and animals.
D.L.

CONTENTS

ACKNOWLEDGEMENTS

I wish to acknowledge the essential support of Heimrath's Raiders: Jean-Marie; Heather Edwards; Sheila Brazys; Melody, Madison, and Peyton Sieger; Leslie Soldat; Jeff Sole; Sarah Andrews; and Gary Mottola.

PREFACE

When I was a young man, someone I worked for told me, "You think too much."

"There's no such thing," I replied.

Then he fired me.

I still believe I was right, and working on the Now You Know series has reaffirmed that conviction. We may not need to know much more than how to catch a bus or start a car to get to work, but when we get there, it's a good idea to have an idea (even if your boss doesn't).

The "Almighty" has generally allocated three original ideas for each human being, so learn how to use them well. All of life is an internship: watching, learning, and then challenging.

As children, we live within dreams, and though these can be either woven or altered by adults, they can never be totally destroyed. It is through this time of innocence that we discover all that will ever be important to us — our minds. You don't live in a nice house, a run-down apartment, or even a mansion; you live in your mind!

All around us, and yes, even within each of us, is the living evidence of the great minds from history. It's in the architecture and monuments, the libraries and galleries, and the marvels of our electronic conveniences. It's in the decaying isolated homes of early settlers and in the walls of ancient forts and castles. It's in our fairy tales, our fashion, our customs, and our art, but most important, it's within our languages, our everyday speech.

This book is the fourth in which I have explored everyday language and customs, and those who have become collectors of these volumes will notice a subtle expansion in content and format. For example, interspersed throughout this book are short features that I call "Odds & Oddities," which present the odds or chances of something. Also scattered throughout the book in relevant places are what I call "Quickies," bite-size bits of information taking the form of "Did you know …?" And from time to time you'll encounter other boxed items such as bumper stickers for baby boomers. Lastly, at the end of this volume, I've answered a selected sample of questions posed by readers of my books.

All of these new elements stay true to the theme of this book's predecessors and comply with my editorial criteria: if it interests me, if it's fun, then it will hopefully amuse and interest you.

Once again I remind you that each gem in this book has been thoroughly researched and is intended to entertain anyone of any age, and who knows, maybe you'll learn something. I did!

Doug Lennox
Toronto, Ontario
June 2006
www.douglennox.com

WORDS
&
EXPRESSIONS

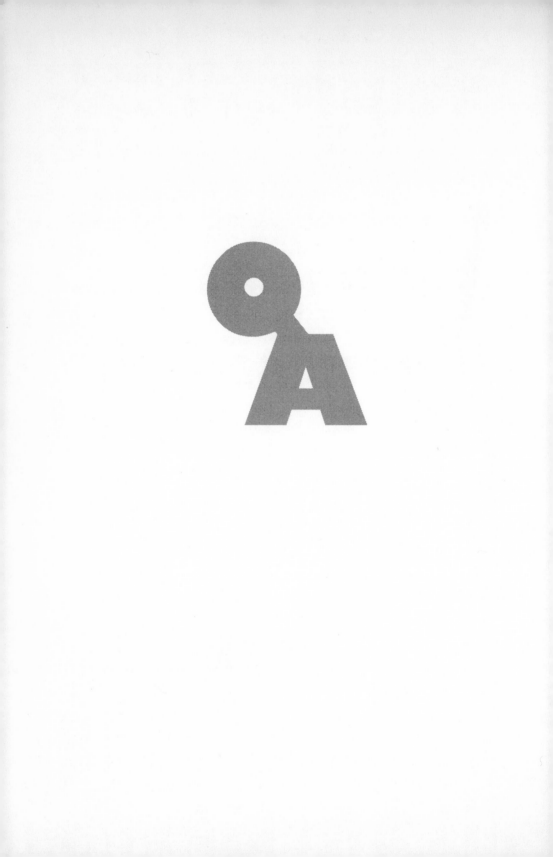

What are the most common words in the English language?

The most common word used in written English is *the*, followed in order of use by *of*, *and*, *to*, *a*, *in*, *that*, *is*, *I*, *it*, *for*, and *as*. The most common spoken English word is *I*. The most common word in the King James Bible is *the*.

Why is relaxing a tense situation called "breaking the ice"?

Overcoming an awkward moment in either business or social circles sometimes requires a little levity to "break the ice" in order to make progress. The expression originally meant to smash the melting ice that hindered commerce during the long winter freeze. It was first used literally in its figurative modern way in 1823 when, in *Don Juan*, Lord Byron (1788–1824) wrote in reference to the stiff British upper class: "And your cold people are beyond all price, when once you've broken their confounded ice."

How did "hightailing it" come to mean a rushed exit?

When people leave in a frantic hurry, they are "hightailing it." The expression grew out of America's Old West after cowboys noticed that both wild horses and deer would jerk their tails up high when frightened as they dashed to safety. The lifting of the tail by both animals was a signal to the rest of the herd that humans, and therefore danger, were near and that the creatures needed to run for their lives.

What is the origin of the expression "hail-fellow-well-met"?

"Hail-fellow-well-met" is an archaic reference to someone who is always cheerful but who is perhaps overdoing his or her enthusiasm. The expression began pleasantly enough as the medieval Scottish greeting *hail*, which is how the Scots pronounced *heal*. "Hale fellow" meant "health to you, friend." In the sixteenth century, the expression became associated with the words *buddy* or *mate*. "Well met!" followed, meaning, "It's good to meet you!" The two expressions became combined in a fuller phrase, "Hail-fellow-well-met," in the late sixteenth century and is used today to suggest that a person's exuberance is perhaps exaggerated.

Exactly What Is a Proverb?

A proverb is an ancient expression of practical truth or wisdom. Proverbs existed before books, were the unwritten language of morality, and are treasures of the oral tradition of all mankind. They offer a deep insight into the everyday domestic life of the culture of their origin and resonate as truth through all time.

Japan:	"Learning without wisdom is a load of books on the back of a jackass."
Japan:	"Unpolished pearls never shine."
England:	"The difference is wide that the sheets cannot decide."
Italy:	"Better alone than in bad company."
China:	"One picture is worth 10,000 words."
Greece:	"He who marries for money, earns it."
Greece:	"If you sleep with dogs, you will arise with fleas."
France:	"He who makes excuses, accuses himself."
Germany:	"He who remains on the floor cannot fall."
Poland:	"The voice is a second face."
Ireland:	"A smile is the whisper of a laugh."
Native American:	"Don't judge someone till you've walked a mile in their moccasins."

Why do we say that something likely to happen soon is "in the offing"?

Something "in the offing" isn't about to happen in the present, or even soon, but it will certainly happen before too long. *Offing* is an early nautical term that describes the part of the ocean most distant from the shore but still visible. So someone who is watching for a ship would first see it in the "offing" and realize that its arrival was imminent.

The phrase "in the offing" was first used during the sixteenth century and began as *offen* or *offin*.

Why is a couched insult called a "backhanded compliment"?

A compliment intended as an insult is termed a "backhanded compliment" and is directly tied to the ancient belief that the left side of the body was under the influence of the devil. A backhanded slap would generally come from the right hand of the majority of people. It is similar to the backhand stroke of tennis players who must reach across their bodies to deliver blows from the left (or evil) side. Anything delivered from the left, including a compliment, was considered sinister or devious.

The word *sinister* comes from *sinestra*, Latin for *left*. Seven percent of the world's population is left-handed. Among the forty-three American presidents, the percentage of lefties is higher (12 percent). Bill Clinton (1946–), George H.W. Bush (1924–), Ronald Reagan (1911–2004), Gerald Ford (1913–), and Harry Truman (1884–1972) are or were left-handed. James Garfield (1831–1881) and Thomas Jefferson (1743–1826) were reportedly ambidextrous.

What is the meaning of "cut to the quick"?

"Cut to the quick" is employed in two ways. It sometimes means (a) "get to the point," or "cut to the chase," but more often it implies (b) "causing deep emotional pain." The *quick* in both cases is the flesh of the finger beneath the nail. Either way the expression means cutting through the inconsequential to the meaningful. An example of (a) would be a combatant cutting through an opponent's armour or clothing to get to the flesh (or point of consequence), while the meaning when used as (b) would be to cut deeply or stab through the superficial exterior (the skin) to a vulnerable part of the body.

"Cut to the quick" is related to the phrase "the quick and the dead." *Quick* here comes from an old English word, *cwicu*, which meant "living."

Where did the expression "bite the dust" come from?

We have probably all heard "bite the dust" for the first time while watching an old western B movie when a cowboy hero does away with a pesky varmint to impress the schoolmarm. The phrase was first used in English literature in 1750 to imply wounding or killing by satirical novelist Tobias Smollett (1721–1771) in *Adventures of Gil Blas of*

Santillane, his translation of the original French novel by Alain-René Lesage: "We made two of them bite the dust and the others betake themselves to flight." The inspiration for the expression can be traced back to the Bible in Psalm 72: "They that dwell in the wilderness shall bow before him and his enemies shall lick the dust."

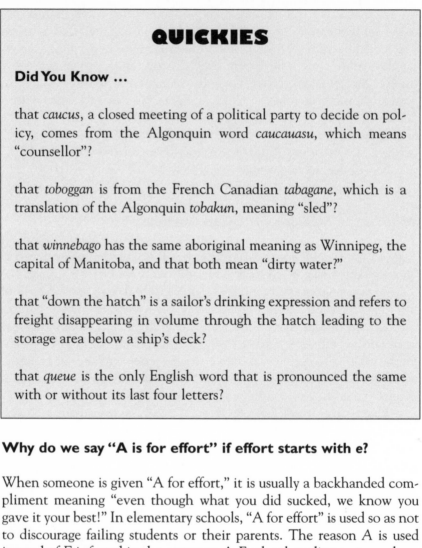

QUICKIES

Did You Know ...

that *caucus*, a closed meeting of a political party to decide on policy, comes from the Algonquin word *caucauasu*, which means "counsellor"?

that *toboggan* is from the French Canadian *tabagane*, which is a translation of the Algonquin *tobakun*, meaning "sled"?

that *winnebago* has the same aboriginal meaning as Winnipeg, the capital of Manitoba, and that both mean "dirty water?"

that "down the hatch" is a sailor's drinking expression and refers to freight disappearing in volume through the hatch leading to the storage area below a ship's deck?

that *queue* is the only English word that is pronounced the same with or without its last four letters?

Why do we say "A is for effort" if effort starts with e?

When someone is given "A for effort," it is usually a backhanded compliment meaning "even though what you did sucked, we know you gave it your best!" In elementary schools, "A for effort" is used so as not to discourage failing students or their parents. The reason A is used instead of *E* is found in the common A-F school grading system where there is no E:˙A = excellent; B = good; C = fair or average; D = poor, but just barely passing; and F = failure.

Why do we say someone is "head over heels" when in love?

When people fall "head over heels" in love, their world has been turned upside down by romance. The word *fallen* suggests helplessness, and the metaphorical "head over heels" is intended to expand the illusion. However, consider that having your head over your heels is, in fact, the normal standing position! You can blame American frontiersman, U.S. congressman, and Alamo martyr Davy Crockett (1786–1836), among others, for turning the phrase around. When the expression first appeared around 1350, it was "heels over head." In his 1834 autobiography, Crockett wrote: "I soon found myself 'head over heels' in love with this girl." So the phrase has been "head over heels" ever since.

What are the meanings of common Yiddish words?

Some familiar Yiddish words are: *chutzpah*, "audacity or boldness"; *schmuck*, "a jerk or a foolish idiot" (literally meaning *schmok*, "penis" or "family jewels"); *klutz*, "a clumsy person"; *putz*, "an unclean, stupid person"; *mensch*, "a good and decent human being"; *l'chaim*, "joyful toast to life"; *schlemiel*, "an inept or incompetent person"; *goy*, "a Gentile, a person who is not Jewish"; *tochis*, "rear end," "butt"; *pisher*, "a male infant, a little squirt, someone of little significance" (yes the word comes from what it sounds like); *shiksa*, "a Gentile woman" (originally this word meant "an abomination"); and *schmooze*, "small talk," usually meaning "sucking up."

Yiddish is a Germanic language and is spoken by about three million people throughout the world. Although the word *Yiddish* is, in fact, Yiddish for "Jewish," it is most likely from the German word *jiddisch*, an abbreviated form of *yidish-taytsh* or "Jewish German." The word came to North America and entered English with immigrants from Central and Eastern Europe at the beginning of the twentieth century.

Mazel tov is well-known for its use at the end of a Jewish wedding ceremony. Often it is thought to be Yiddish, but actually it comes from *mazzāl*, which means "star" in Hebrew. *Mazel tov* is used as "congratulations," but literally means "may you be born under a good star." After telling someone *mazel tov*, it's customary to shake hands.

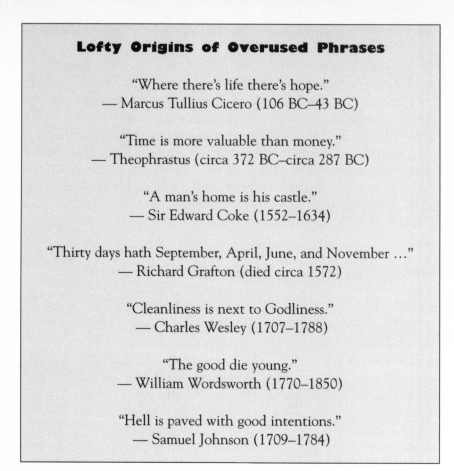

Lofty Origins of Overused Phrases

"Where there's life there's hope."
— Marcus Tullius Cicero (106 BC–43 BC)

"Time is more valuable than money."
— Theophrastus (circa 372 BC–circa 287 BC)

"A man's home is his castle."
— Sir Edward Coke (1552–1634)

"Thirty days hath September, April, June, and November ..."
— Richard Grafton (died circa 1572)

"Cleanliness is next to Godliness."
— Charles Wesley (1707–1788)

"The good die young."
— William Wordsworth (1770–1850)

"Hell is paved with good intentions."
— Samuel Johnson (1709–1784)

How did the word *moron* come to mean "stupid"?

We have all been called a moron at one time or another and under-
stood it to mean we've done something foolish. The reason is that in
1910 Dr. Henry H. Goddard (1866–1957) proposed the word to the
American Association for the Study of the Feebleminded to describe
an adult with the mental capacity (IQ below 75) of a normal child
between eight and twelve years of age. A moron was, in fact, the
highest proposed rating of a mentally challenged person. The two
lowest ratings suggested were imbecile and idiot. These categories
have been dropped by the scientific community and are no longer in
use — except as an insult!

Moron is from the Greek *moros*, meaning "stupid" or "foolish."

Why does the word *bully* have both good and bad meanings?

Today a bully is generally a description of a brute who intimidates someone weaker or more vulnerable, but in the United States the positive power of the presidency is often referred to as the "bully pulpit." In the 1500s, the word in its positive sense entered English from the Dutch *boel*, meaning "sweetheart" or "brother," but by the 1700s, the word's meaning deteriorated when it became the popular description of a pimp who protected his prostitutes with violence.

In North America, distanced by the ocean, the word stayed closer to its positive origins and gave rise to the expression "bully for you," meaning "admirable or worthy of praise."

Why are rental accommodations called "digs"?

Digs comes from Australian gold prospectors who used the word *diggings* to describe their mining claims, which usually included makeshift lodgings. In 1893 *digs* first appeared as a slang term for rooms and small apartments in boarding houses that were strictly supervised by landladies who usually forbade visits by the opposite sex. Students have since adopted the word to describe the humble temporary places they call home.

Why do we say that somebody who speaks nonsense is "babbling"?

To babble means to speak foolishness. It is a verb rooted in the French and Scandinavian languages and was used to describe baby talk in the months leading up to a child's first words. *Babble* has many different forms and circumstances, for example, *squabble*, *blather*, and *charlatan*, all of which, to some degree, mean "chattering and prattling nonsense."

The Latin for *babble* is *blatire*. *Babble* or *blatire* is the word that *blatant* is derived from. It was coined by English poet Edmund Spenser (1552–1599) in *The Faerie Queene* in 1596 to describe a thousand-tongued beast representing slander.

ARTS
&
ENTERTAINMENT

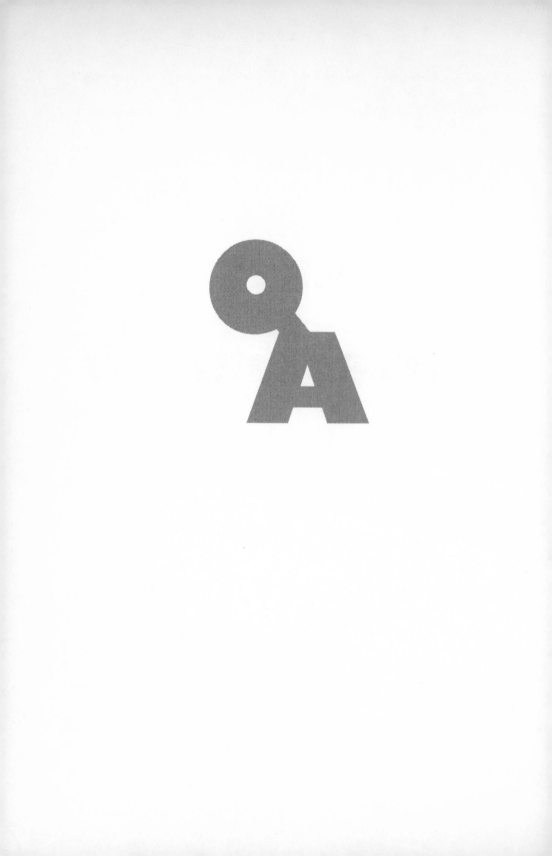

Why do we refer to a tired story or joke as an "old chestnut"?

If a joke or expression works, especially for a comic or a public speaker, it is usually overused and is consequently called "an old chestnut." The expression comes from a British play, *The Broken Sword, or The Torrent of the Valley*, written by William Dimond (1780–1837) and first produced in 1816 at London's Royal Covent Garden Theatre. Within that play a principal character continually repeats the same joke about a cork tree, each time with a subtle variation, including changing the tree from cork to chestnut. Finally, tiring of the joke, another character, Pablo, says: "A chestnut! I've heard you tell that joke twenty-seven times and I'm sure it was a chestnut!"

The impact moment when the phrase likely entered the English language was during a dinner party somewhat later in the nineteenth century. At the dinner the American actor William Warren the Younger (1812–1888), who at the time was playing the part of Pablo, used the "chestnut line" from the play to interrupt a guest who had begun to repeat an old familiar joke. Coincidentally perhaps, the younger Warren's father, also named William, was an actor, too, who for a time was associated with Philadelphia's Chestnut Street Theater.

Why is an artist's inspiration called a "muse"?

Many great artists have been influenced by a muse, a person whose very existence inspires them to reach beyond themselves. It literally means the inspiration a man receives from a special woman. The word *muse*, as it is used in this case, comes from any of the nine beautiful daughters of Mnemosyne and Zeus, each of whom in Greek mythology presided over a different art or science. *Muse* is the derivative of such words as *music*, *museum*, and *mosaic*.

The Greek Muses also gave us the English word *muzzle*, because before *muse* entered English around 1380 it was known in Old French as *muser*, "to ponder or loiter," usually with your nose in the air (something all artists are familiar with). Before that the derivative in Gallo-Romance was *musa* or "snout."

Muse	Art or Science	Symbol
Calliope	Epic poetry	Tablet and stylus/scroll
Clio	History	Open chest of books
Erato	Love and poetry	Lyre
Euterpe	Lyric poetry	Flute
Melpomene	Tragedy	Tragic mask
Polyhymnia	Sacred poetry	None; she sits pensively
Terpsichore	Choral song and dance	Lyre
Thalia	Comedy	Comic mask/wreath of ivy
Urania	Astronomy	Staff pointing to a globe

Why is making it up as you go called "winging it"?

"Winging it" usually implies the same thing as having your first swimming lesson by being thrown into the deep end of a pool. It takes courage and sometimes ability you didn't know you had. It's an exercise familiar to good salespeople. The expression derives from an unprepared stage actor standing in the "wings" and cramming desperately before hearing a cue that will force him onstage.

QUICKIES

Did You Know ...

that playing cards in Spanish are called *tarjeta*, meaning "little shields"?

that "no dice," meaning "no deal," comes from a time when dice were tossed during a game and either didn't land flat or were thrown out of play?

that "egg on your face" means to look foolish or embarrassed and comes from bad actors having eggs thrown at them by the audience?

that "one potato, two potato, three potato, four," the children's counting-rhyme, originated in Canada around 1885?

How did "Greensleeves" become a Christmas song?

The ballad "Greensleeves" was first published in 1580, but no doubt had been known long before that. One early lyric ("Lady Greensleeves") was a love song to a well-dressed woman, possibly a prostitute. The music's first application to Christmas appeared in *New Christmas Carols of 1642* and was entitled "The Old Year Now Is Fled." William Dix, a British insurance agent, wrote a poem in 1865 entitled "The Manger Throne." In 1872 a publisher took three of the poem's many verses, set them to the "Greensleeves" melody, and published the resulting song as "What Child Is This?"

Contrary to a popular legend, England's King Henry VIII (1491–1547) did not write the music for "Greensleeves."

The song has been around for 500 years and has been used to cover a myriad of lyrics within almost as many different theatrical productions and has even been referenced by William Shakespeare (1564–1616). Its most successful modern secular rendition was as the theme for the 1962 John Ford (1895–1973) movie *How the West Was Won*.

Why do jazz musicians call a spontaneous collaboration a "jam"?

All musicians refer to an informal and exhilarating musical session as "jamming," but the term first surfaced in the jazz world during the 1920s. "Jam" in jazz is a short, free, improvised passage performed by the whole band. It means pushing or "jamming" all the players and notes into a defined free-flowing session. And just like the preserved fruit "jammed" into a jar, a musical jam is sweet!

Preserved fruit was first called jam during the 1730s simply because it was crushed, then "jammed" into a jar. To be "in a jam" has the same origin and means to be pressed into a tight or confining predicament. *Jamming* radio signals is a term from World War I and means to force so much extra sound through a defined enemy channel that the original intended message is incoherent. All this is from *jam*, a little seventeenth-century word of unknown origin that meant to press tightly.

Who is the "Thinker" in Auguste Rodin's famous statue?

The French sculptor Auguste Rodin's statue commonly called *The Thinker* (*Le penseur*) is one of the best-known pieces of art in the world. Yet when Rodin (1840–1917) first cast a small plaster version in 1880, he meant it as a depiction of the Italian poet Dante Alighieri (circa 1265–1321) pondering his great allegorical epic *The Divine Comedy* in front of the Gates of Hell. In fact, Rodin named the sculpture *The Poet*. It was an obscure critic, unfamiliar with Dante, who misnamed the masterpiece with the title we use today — *The Thinker*.

Rodin's statue is naked because the sculptor wanted a heroic classical figure to represent Thought as Poetry.

How did the Romans use "thumbs up" and "thumbs down" in the Coliseum?

Ancient Roman spectators in the Coliseum did use their thumbs to show their decisions on whether a losing gladiator should live or die, but not in the manner we see expressed today. It was the movies that gave us the simple "thumbs up or thumbs down." The thumb symbolized the weapon of the victor. "Up" meant "lift your sword and let him live." But if the verdict was death, then the thumb was thrust forward and downward in a stabbing motion.

What is the weight of the Academy of Motion Picture Arts and Sciences' prized Oscar?

Recipients of the Academy Award, commonly known as the Oscar, always seem to be surprised at its weight. The Oscar was designed in 1928 by Cedric Gibbons (1893–1960), Metro-Goldwyn-Mayer's chief art director. The statuette depicts a knight standing on a reel of film and holding a crusader sword. Originally, Oscar was made of gold-plated bronze. Today the base of the twenty-four-karat gold-plated britannium statuette is black marble. Oscar is 13.5 inches tall and weighs 8.5 pounds.

Why is a glitzy sales presentation called a "dog and pony show"?

In the late 1800s, shows featuring small animals began touring little North American farming towns that weren't on the larger circuses' itineraries. These travelling shows were made up of dogs and ponies that did tricks. Some, like the Gentry Brothers Circus, were very successful, using up to eighty dogs and forty ponies in a single show. Over time the expression "dog and pony show" became a negative description for anything small-time and sleazy, like a low-budget sales presentation that's heavy on glitz and light on substance.

How did the Ferris wheel get its name?

The first Ferris wheel was built by and named after George Washington Gale Ferris (1859–1896) and was constructed as an attraction for the 1893 World's Columbian Exposition in Chicago. Ferris had set out to

build a structure that would rival the Eiffel Tower built four years earlier for the Paris Exposition. The two towers that supported the wheel
were 140 feet high, the wheel itself was 250 feet across, and the top of
the structure was 264 feet above the ground. It held more than 2,000
passengers, cost $380,000 to build, and earned more than $725,000
during the fair.

Unlike the Eiffel Tower, which survived plans for its demolition
when it proved useful as a communications tower, the first Ferris wheel
was destroyed in 1906.

What is unique about the Beatles song "Yesterday"?

"Yesterday" has had more airtime than any other song in history. The
Beatles' Paul McCartney (1942–) said the song came to him in a
dream. While writing it he used the working title "Scrambled Eggs."
When McCartney recorded the song in 1965, none of the other
Beatles were in the studio. He was alone with his guitar and a group of
string musicians. Since the release of "Yesterday," more than 3,000 versions of it have been recorded.

Why were teenage girls once called "bobbysoxers"?

Frank Sinatra (1915–1998) was the first pop singer to experience primal
teenage female screaming and tearful shrieking during a musical perform-
ance. These legions of young women and girls were called bobbysoxers
because they were the first generation to wear short or cutoff stockings,
leaving their nubile bare legs to disappear beneath a shorter rather than
longer skirt. "Bobby socks" or "bobbed socks" first appeared in the 1930s
and were so called because they had been cut short. "Bobbed" meant "cut
short" like the tail of a "bobtailed nag" or a woman's "bobbed hair."

Teenager was a new word during the time of the bobbysoxers.

Nubile had always meant "marriageable" until 1973 when it came
to mean "sexually attractive."

Why is the children's play kit known as LEGO?

LEGO is a trademark name for a child's plastic construction set derived
from a 1934 invention by a humble and struggling Danish carpenter

named Ole Kirk Christiansen (1891–1958). The company name LEGO comes from the Danish words *leg godt*, meaning "play well." There is a myth that Christiansen didn't realize that *lego* in Latin means "I assemble." In fact, the word in Latin means "I read" and has nothing to do with the legend or the truth of the play kit or the company's name. The motto on the wall of Christiansen's carpentry workshop was Only the Best Is Good Enough.

Why is foolish behaviour called "tomfoolery"?

A buffoon was first called a "Tom fool" in 1650 because Tom was a nickname for a "common man." Although *fool* once meant "mad" or "insane," by the seventeenth century it was a reference to a jester or a clown. The name Tom became influenced by "Tom the cat" in the 1809 popular children's book *The Life and Adventures of a Cat*. Tom the cat was quite silly and was a promiscuous night crawler. This all led to *tomfoolery* becoming a word for crazy behaviour.

Another Tom phrase was "Tom o' Bedlam," the nickname given to the insane men who, because of overcrowding and spiralling costs, had been released from London's Bethlehem or "Bedlam" Hospital for the Insane and were given a licence to beg on the streets. (The term is also a dig at the Irish). Bedlam is a cockney pronunciation of Bethlehem.

Where does the Sandman come from?

The Sandman is an elf who sprinkles sand in children's eyes to make them sleepy. The character is derived from the remarkable mind of Hans Christian Andersen (1805–1875), the Danish writer famous for his fairy tales. Andersen's Sandman was a device to explain to children the reason for the grit or "sleep" in their eyes when they woke up in the morning. The Sandman is found in Andersen's 1850 story "Ole Lukoie," which means "Olaf Shuteye." Olaf carried two umbrellas. Over good children he held an umbrella with pictures that inspired beautiful dreams. Over bad children he held the other umbrella, which had no pictures and caused frightful dreams.

Andersen was born in the slums of Odense, Denmark, and his incredible life story is well worth reading for inspiration.

FASHION

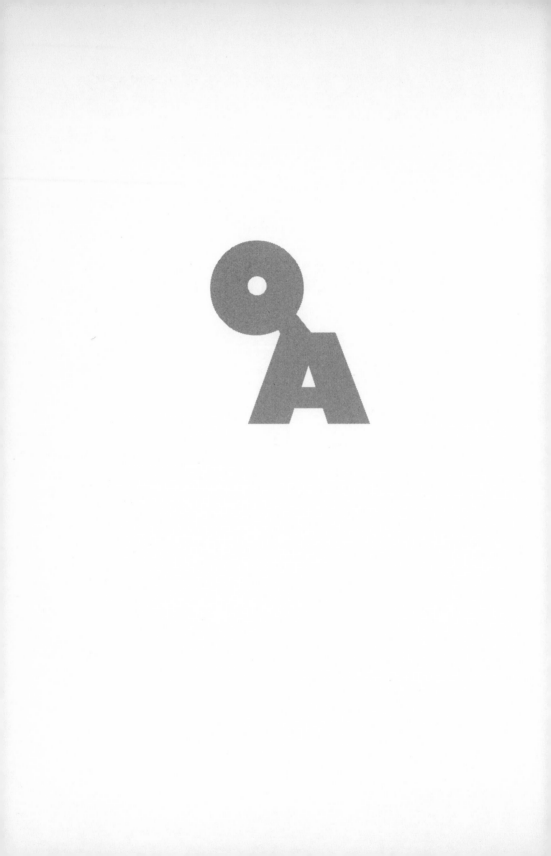

Why does "lace" describe an ornamental fabric and a string for tying shoes?

The word *lace* began its route into thirteenth-century English as the Latin word *lacere*, which means "to entice." On its way through Spanish and French, *lace* became a hunting term meaning "rope net," "snare," or "noose." In 1555, because fancy lace reminded someone of a hunting net, the word *lace* was employed to describe an ornamental netted fabric pattern and, shortly after, as a cord for tying, such as a shoelace. As its use in hunting diminished, *lace* or "netting" took on the primary meaning of "ornamental trim."

The expression "to lace a drink" by adding a dash of liquor derived from the new habit of adding sugar to coffee or tea during the seventeenth century, and also meant "ornamental trim."

The Spanish word for a "hunting lace" or a rope was *lazo*, which gave cowboys the lasso.

"Laced mutton" was an old expression for a prostitute.

Why do we call women's underwear "bloomers"?

In the mid-nineteenth century, Mrs. Elizabeth Smith Miller (1822–1911) revolutionized women's wear by designing and wearing a clothing style that did away with voluminous dresses and tightly laced corsets. She suggested that women wear a jacket and knee-length skirt over a pair of

trousers tucked into boots. The cause was taken up by magazine editor and feminist Amelia Jenks Bloomer (1818–1894) and was given a boost by the new pastime of bicycling. There was a lot of resistance before the new dress became acceptable and took the name of its most visible advocate, Amelia Bloomer.

Bloomers soon became applied to just the trousers and eventually to any sort of long underwear.

Why is a light, short overcoat called a "jacket"?

A short coat is called a jacket for the same reason that Jack is used generically to mean any male stranger ("hit the road, Jack"). It was the French who began using Jacques this way as a reference to any common or unsophisticated male. The word took on the meaning of a peasant or ordinary man's outerwear in France and spread throughout Europe, arriving in England as *jacket* during the thirteenth century.

As a nickname for John, Jack is used as an endearment like "buddy" or "mate" and has been since the days of Middle English. During this same time, Dicken became popular as the original nickname for Richard until it evolved into Dick, while Robin was an endearment for Robert before it became Rob.

Why do we say that someone well dressed wore his or her best "bib and tucker"?

In the seventeenth century, bibs were introduced to protect men's clothing from the consequences of their own bad table manners. Women did the same, but their bibs were fancier and were made of lace or muslin with frills to frame their faces. Because these bibs were tucked into the tops of low-cut dresses, they were called tuckers. On special occasions both men and women brought their own bibs and tuckers to the banquet and, just like their clothing, these made a fashion statement.

How did the bowler hat become an English icon?

The caricature of an Englishman used to include an umbrella, a briefcase, and a bowler hat. Although this is an outdated image, it still recalls a class system that defines the British character. The first bowler was designed in the mid-1800s by London hatters James and George Lock as a protective riding hat for Thomas William Coke. The headgear became synonymous with property owners and consequently the gentry or well-to-do. The hat got its name from Thomas and William Bowler, the hat-makers who produced Coke's prototype.

Americans call this hat a derby, probably because it was so prevalent within the wealthy compound at major horse races.

Winston Churchill (1874–1965) was one of the last of his generation to make the bowler high fashion.

London's trademark black high-roofed taxicabs were designed so that gentlemen wouldn't have to remove their bowlers.

Why is a type of woman's underwear called a "G-string"?

Although our prehistoric ancestors wore leather loincloths that have been excavated from more than 7,000 years ago, underwear as we know it didn't become "normal" until the thirteenth century when it was tied at the waist and knees. The ancient Greeks didn't wear underwear, though their slaves sported a kind of loincloth. The G in G-string stands for "groin" and was first used to describe the loincloths worn by North American Natives. As women's wear, G-strings first appeared in the 1930s when they were the exclusive attire of strippers.

LAW & ORDER

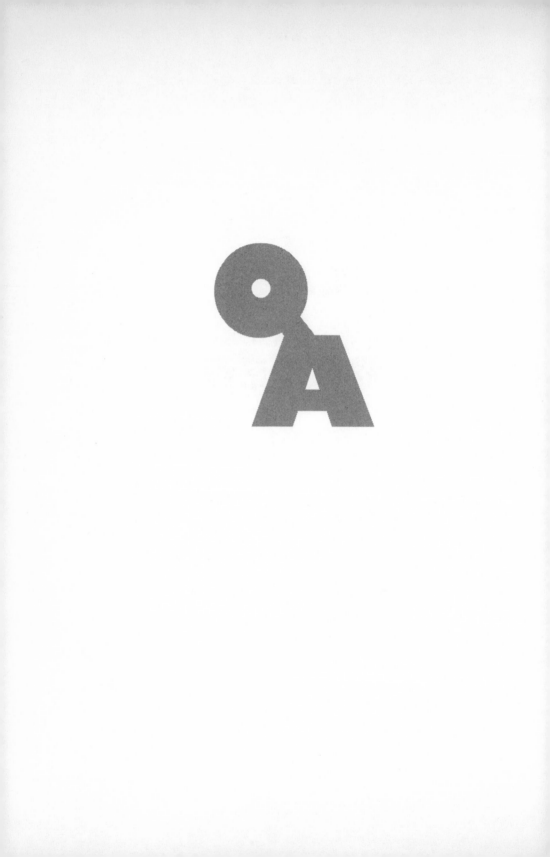

Why is a lie or a deception called a "falsehood"?

A falsehood is a lie or a distortion of the truth and derives from a time before men wore hats. They used hoods to cover their heads from the elements, and these hoods were designed with fur or something else to indicate an individual's rank within the community. If a con man wished to deceive you, he put on a hood designed to be worn by a person of substance such as a doctor or a lawyer. This tactic enabled him to gain enough trust to set up an illegal scam. The con man did this by wearing a "false hood."

Why do we say someone has been "fired" when he or she is forced out of a job?

Being fired is usually unpleasant, and even though it's sometimes a disguised blessing, it never reaches the cruelty of its medieval Celtic origins. If a clan leader wanted to get rid of a petty criminal without killing him, or if someone was found guilty of stealing from his employer, especially from the mines, he was taken to his home along with all his tools and placed inside after which the house was "fired" or set on fire. If he escaped, he was banished from the clan.

Why is a useless conclusion to an argument called "moot"?

If, after an argument, it is concluded that the point made is irrelevant, it's called moot. Moot is an Old English word that means "an assembly of the people for making judicial or political decisions." That's how the word took on the meaning of a discussion or a debate. By the sixteenth century, moot had developed the specific meaning within the legal profession of a "hypothetical discussion on a legal point as an intellectual exercise."

Just as arguments at an original moot or town meeting were of little consequence, the conclusions of an academic exercise among lawyers carries no weight in the real world and so it, too, is irrelevant or moot.

What is "trial by combat"?

Today "trial by combat" is generally used as a reference to lessons learned through experience, such as a soldier who has seen action, but the term was, in fact, from a legitimate legal process also known as "judicial combat." In medieval Christian cultures it was agreed that God decided the outcome of trials, a belief that rooted such proceedings in the legal theory of "ordeals": torture tests that God would see you through if you were innocent.

Trial by combat was practised by the nobility and by military courts under the guise of chivalry while commoners were tried by ordeal. The court determined a just outcome by sentencing the plaintiff and defendant to a trial by combat, a legal fight, often to the death, with the survivor or victor to be chosen by God. Trial by combat, or judicial combat, was usually the settlement of one man's word against that of another. Most of these duels were fought over a question of honour and were most frequently performed in France up until the late sixteenth century.

In 1833, twenty-three-year-old John Wilson killed nineteen-year-old Robert Lyon of Perth, Ontario, in what was the last recorded mortal duel in Canada. Wilson later became a judge in the Ontario Supreme Court.

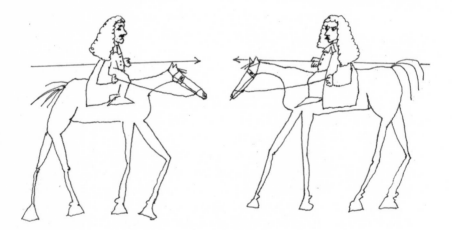

Why do we sometimes say "fork it over" in place of "hand it over"?

The expression "fork it over" has a connotation of urgency to it and is often used dramatically during a criminal holdup. In fact, the expression does have origins in a long-forgotten underworld. Of course, the phrase can also be employed with humour when asking for a financial payment for goods or services rendered or for the repayment of a loan. The "fork" in question is a reference to "fingers," which were the original dinner forks, especially for thieves and other low-lifes.

Why is a monetary deposit for freedom from prison called "bail"?

A bailiff is a sheriff's deputy, a subordinate magistrate with jurisdiction over a strictly defined area. He or she has responsibility over the custody and administration of prisoners. To the early English, *bailiff* meant "village" and derived from *bail*, which described the palisade or wall around a community or castle. *Bailey* came to mean any wall enclosing an outer court, and because the Central Criminal Court in London stood within the ancient bailey of the city wall, it took the name Old Bailey. Monetary bail for restricted freedom is simply a reference to the bailiff's office.

Bail, the root for *bailiff*, originally meant a "horizontal piece of wood affixed to two stakes," as in the case of the wicket in the game of cricket.

Why is support paid by one former spouse to another called "alimony"?

The court often orders the chief provider of a divorcing couple to pay an allowance to the other. This sum of money is called alimony because it literally keeps the recipient alive. In Latin *alimony* means "nourishment" or "sustenance."

The term *palimony* was coined in 1979 to apply to the separation of film star Lee Marvin (1924–1987) from a long-time live-in lover. Palimony applies the same rules to an unmarried couple who have coexisted equally and contributed to the couple's success.

Why is land called "real estate"?

Real estate is a piece of land that includes the air above it, the ground below it, and any buildings or structures on it. The term was first used in 1666 England. In 1670 the word *realty* surfaced to mean the same thing. *Real* means "actual" or "genuine," and *estate*, of course, means "property." Real estate became a legal term to identify a royal grant of estate land from the king of England.

In England a real-estate broker or realtor is called a land agent.

ODDS & ODDITIES

The odds of being the victim of a serious crime in one's lifetime are 20 to 1.

The odds of being murdered are 18,000 to 1, with the chance of being the victim of a sharp or blunt instrument being six times greater than from a gun for which the odds against that occurring are 325 to 1.

The chance of dying from an assault of any kind is 1 in 16,421.

The odds of getting away with murder are 2 to 1.

Why are private detectives called "gumshoes"?

Around the beginning of the twentieth century a popular casual shoe was manufactured with a sole made of gum rubber. They were very quiet and were favoured by thieves who used them during burglaries and other crimes and consequently became required footwear for the detectives hunting them down. The term *gumshoe* stuck with private detectives as it aptly described the stealthy and secretive nature of their work.

Why are informers called "whistle-blowers"?

A whistle-blower is an insider who secretly reveals nefarious or scandalous wrongdoing by an organization or a government. The reference is, of course, to a referee or umpire who calls a foul during a sporting event. It was introduced to our vernacular in 1953 by the American writer Raymond Chandler (1888–1959) in his Philip Marlowe detective novel *The Long Goodbye*.

The most famous whistle-blower of the twentieth century was Deep Throat, who revealed the criminal inner workings of the administration of President Richard Nixon (1913–1994) during the Watergate break-in affair. In 2005 the identity of Deep Throat was finally made public. He was W. Mark Felt (1913–), the former assistant director of the Federal Bureau of Investigation during Nixon's presidency.

Why do we threaten to read the "riot act" to discipline children?

In law a riot is "a violent disturbance of the public peace by twelve or more persons assembled for a common purpose" and may be committed in private as well as public places. The Riot Act, which carried real weight and is the one we still refer to in the expression, became law in England in 1714. It authorized the death penalty for those who failed to disperse after the act had been formally read to those assembled. Thankfully, there have been modern revisions to that act, though the consequences to those who disobey the order to disband can still be severe. Children beware!

WAR
&
THE MILITARY

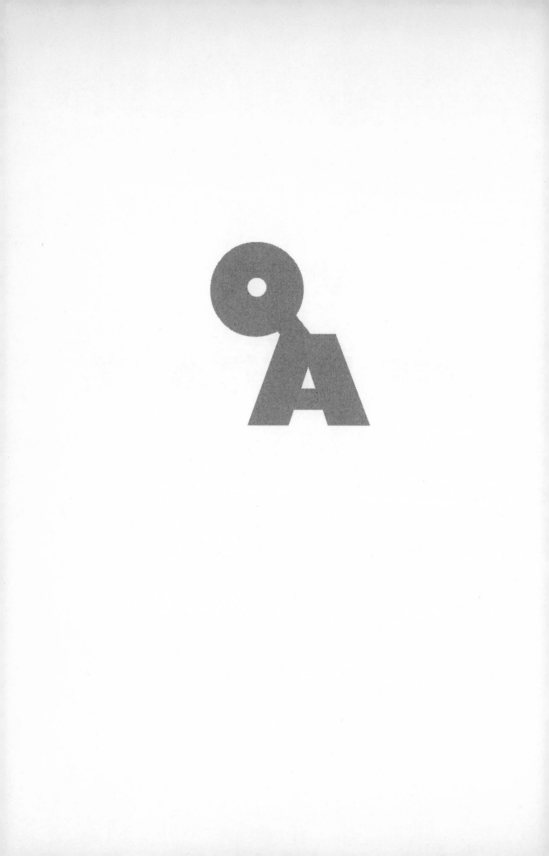

What is the unique story behind the Victoria Cross?

The United Kingdom's Queen Victoria created the Victoria Cross in 1856 to recognize individual acts of gallantry by soldiers and sailors of the British Empire. The new medal came on the heels of, and was inspired by, the heroics of the Crimean War fought by Britain, France, the Kingdom of Sardinia, and the Ottoman Empire against Russia between 1854 and 1856. To this day each Victoria Cross is forged from the melted-down metal of Russian cannon captured during the Crimean War. Unlike some other British medals, the Victoria Cross can be awarded to any member of the military regardless of rank. To date, at the time of this writing, 1,355 people have received the medal.

Who were the first and last Canadian recipients of the Victoria Cross?

On August 9, 1945, navy pilot Lieutenant Robert Hampton Gray became the ninety-fourth, and last, Canadian to win the Victoria Cross. He was awarded the medal posthumously for bravery during an attack on a Japanese destroyer on the final day of World War II. The first Canadian to receive the medal was Lieutenant Alexander Roberts Dunn, who won his for bravery during the Charge of the Light Brigade in 1854 at the Battle of Balaclava in the Crimean War.

Canada's last living Victoria Cross recipient was Ernest Alvia "Smokey" Smith, who died at his home in Vancouver in August 2005. Smith, who won his medal in Italy in October 1944, single-handedly saved his company from a German counterattack by three tanks, two self-propelled guns, and thirty infantrymen.

Why is someone of key importance to a team leader called a "right-hand man"?

The term *right-hand man* refers to someone indispensable to the person in charge and derives from the military. Today, when soldiers line up on a parade square, they are copying the alignment employed when armies used to face, then approach, each other in lines for mortal or pitched combat. The tallest or "right-marker" is the first called into position, and all others line up in a sequence of diminishing height to his left. The right-marker is the anchor and reference for all verbal commands off whom the other soldiers react both on the parade square and during battle.

A line of soldiers is called a "pitch."

Why, when we want someone to hurry, do we say "on the double"?

In civilian life "on the double" means to do something in a hurry. In the military, where the expression originated, it is usually a clear command most commonly barked by a drill sergeant ordering his men to do a task "on the double," meaning to "stop walking and start running." Just as bugles were used to relay drills to soldiers in the field, drums were utilized on ships to summon sailors to their battle stations. *Double* was an early reference to increase the drumbeat appropriately to convey urgency to all hands.

What is a "Mexican standoff"?

The classical Mexican standoff occurs when three people level guns at one another in such a way that if one gunman shoots a member of the

trio the person not being shot at will in all likelihood kill the first shooter. In other words, a stalemate ensues. It's a no-win situation. The expression's roots are in the American West where conflicts with the original Mexican settlers were often resolved with guns and even war, which is how Texas, New Mexico, and California became part of the United States. The term *Mexican standoff* came out of these struggles as an ethnic slur, just as *gringo* arose as an epithet for the other side.

Why is a lightning-quick military attack called a "raid"?

A sudden "raid" is usually over quickly, with the attackers strategically withdrawing as soon as their mission is completed. It's always a surprise attack. Consider that the words *road* and *rode* both come from *ride*, as in horseback riding, and then consider that lightning-quick surprise attacks resulted from horsemen charging down a road. *Rade*, "a riding, journey," is the Old English and Scottish derivative word for *raid*. When a hostile incursion came galloping down the road, the cry of "Rade!" went up, which easily became "Raid!" when retold in literature.

Where in the world were highways designed to be emergency "landing strips" during war?

Some highway systems are designed for use as landing strips, but they aren't in North America. There is a legend that the Eisenhower Interstate System in the United States requires one mile in every five to be straight so that it can be used as an airstrip during wartime, but no such law exists either in the United States or Canada. However, the highway systems of South Korea and Sweden have been designed with air war in mind.

Why do we say that someone is too old to "cut the mustard"?

The phrase "too old to cut the mustard" was popularized by a hit song during the 1940s when military expressions were uppermost in the minds of returning servicemen. Simply put, it means that one's "salad days" are in the past. *Mustard* is a mispronunciation of the military word *muster*, which means "inspection." If a soldier doesn't "cut or pass muster," he or she doesn't make the grade. In effect, the soldier fails to pass inspection.

Why is a military dining hall called a "mess"?

A mess hall is what military types call their dining halls. The term's origins go back to the Middle Ages when British sailors began calling their meagre, often grub-infested meals a mess, which they clearly were. *Mess* originally meant the food for one meal. It has since evolved to signify a specific area where sailors, soldiers, and aircrew gather to eat, drink, and socialize.

In order to maintain discipline, there are usually three levels of mess: officers, non-commissioned officers (sergeants), and rank-and-file soldiers.

Why do we say it's a "siege" when an army surrounds a fort or town?

The word *siege* conjures up visions of intense combat, with one force attacking a surrounded enemy with total and absolute ferocity. So it's interesting to note that *siege* means "sit." This origin is illustrated in the Arthurian legends where the "siege perilous" was a vacant seat at the Round Table. The seat was supposed to be fatal to any except the knight destined to find the Holy Grail. Since the thirteenth century, the military sense of *siege* has meant an army "sitting down" around a fortress to wait for those inside to surrender.

Siege came to English through Old French as *sege*, meaning "seat" or "throne," and originated with *sedere*, the Latin word for *sit*. *Siege* is also related to *sedentary*.

What do "razor" and "raze" have in common?

When a man shaves, he uses a razor, so why when soldiers destroy a town do we say they "razed" it to the ground? *Raze* is often employed to describe the results of a fire, not because it has anything to do with flames but simply because there's nothing left. The term's origins began in the fourteenth century when the French word *raser* entered English to describe the morning ritual of shaving. The word meant to scrape, slash, or erase the hair from one's face, just as when an army razes a town it knocks down all of the buildings and levels the settlement to the ground. An anonymous quotation from the Vietnam War puts *raze* into context: "It takes a village to raise a child, but it takes a B-52 to raze a village."

Who first said "damn the torpedoes, full speed ahead!"?

A torpedo can be a number of things, but it's best known as a self-propelled armed tube fired from a submarine. The word was first recorded as an explosive device for blowing up ships in 1776. The word *torpedo* derives from the Latin *torpere*, which means "to numb." During the American Civil War, while he was attacking the Confederates at Mobile Bay, Alabama, in 1864, Admiral David G. Farragut (1801–1879) had his lead ship sunk by a floating mine. In the ensuing confusion, he uttered the famous words: "Damn the torpedoes, full speed ahead!"

What is the meaning of the word *Humvee*?

Humvee is a trademark for a durable wide-bodied military vehicle with four-wheel drive that was developed by American Motors in 1983 to replace the Jeep. The name Humvee is a rough military acronym that came out of the 1991 Gulf War. It means high-mobility multipurpose wheeled vehicle. Substantially larger than the Jeep, the Humvee was able to replace several other vehicles, as well. Since 2000, General Motors has been selling civilian versions of the vehicle.

Why, after a close call, do we say someone has "dodged a bullet"?

You can't get much closer to danger than "dodging a bullet." At close range nobody dodges a bullet, or so it would seem. The expression derives from soldiers in World War I who talked about artillery shells that could be avoided because they arced through the air slowly enough to be seen. The odds of getting out of the way of rifle fire improved as the distance increased, because if you saw the muzzle flash, you had a second or two to move before the bullet got to you. Light travels faster than a bullet!

How close do you have to be before seeing the "whites of their eyes"?

"Don't shoot till you see the whites of their eyes" has echoed through history as an order for soldiers to hold their fire and their nerve until the last minute. At the Battle of Bunker Hill in June 1775 during the American Revolution, a U.S. colonel named William Prescott said it to his men. Before then Prince Charles of Prussia issued the order at the Battle of Jägerndorf in 1757, and Frederick the Great (1712–1786) said it at the Battle of Prague the same year. At the Plains of Abraham in Quebec in 1759, General James Wolfe (1727–1759) told his men not to fire until they saw the whites of their eyes, which meant "hold" until the enemy was fifteen or twenty paces away, a distance of thirty to forty feet.

Why is the truth referred to as "the real skinny"?

The word skinny came to mean "emaciated" around 1605, and during World War II, it began to suggest something that was true. The expression means "let's cut to the bare bones of a situation without any embellishment." In combat there is no time for anything except the "naked truth," so eventually a creative and expedient new slang, "the real skinny," arose.

"Skinny-dip" has the same derivative as "the real skinny" and first appeared in the 1950s.

Where do we get the expression "bang for the buck"?

"Bang for the buck" means getting the most for the amount you have paid. The phrase is a Cold War military expression with sinister suggestions of atomic and other explosive devices. Before the Berlin Wall came down in 1989, the United States and its allies in the West were engaged in a series of confrontations and skirmishes with the former Soviet Union and its satellite states. "Bang for the buck" described how efficiently the American defence (and offence) budgets were being spent.

As poet and playwright T.S. Eliot (1888–1965) wrote in "The Hollow Men" in 1925, "This is the way the world ends/Not with a bang but a whimper."

What are you doing when you "pillage and plunder" while "ransacking" a village?

The Vikings were good at "ransacking" during raids on Britain and other countries, so they gave us the word ransack, which started out meaning to search a house, legally or otherwise, for goods, stolen or otherwise. *Pillage* and *plunder* are almost interchangeable, with *pillage* strictly referring to searching a home for booty, while *plunder* denotes removing what you find.

Whether your home has been searched by the police or a burglar, or a Viking, it's bound to be a mess because it's been ransacked.

Why is a risky mission said to be flown "on a wing and a prayer"?

If someone is operating "on a wing and a prayer," whatever they are doing involves serious risk. The expression became popular with fliers on dangerous missions during World War II and was derived from the song "Comin' in on a Wing and a Prayer," which tells of landing a damaged aircraft. The tune was written in 1943 by Harold Adamson (1906–1980), who also penned "A Lovely Way to Spend an Evening," "Winter Wonderland," and the theme song for the television sitcom *I Love Lucy*. The lyrics of "Comin' in on a Wing and a Prayer" include the title line, which was taken from an actual cockpit transmission from a damaged bomber attempting to land.

PEOPLE

Why is an important person called the "big cheese"?

The "big cheese" is the person with the authority and responsibility for everything within an organization. In this case, *cheese* is an Anglicization of *chiz*, the Urdu word for *thing*. In colonial India, the natives picked up the pre-existing English idiom "the real thing" and made it "the real chiz," which in turn was carried home by the British where to homeland ears *chiz* sounded like *cheese*. In the United States, the "real cheese" was converted to the "big cheese" to describe the most important person in a group.

Who, by profession, make the best tippers?

A recent survey of North American service workers rated the best tippers in this order: (1) Other restaurant workers (2) Regular customers, especially cigarette smokers (3) Young male "wannabes" (4) Small business owners (5) Tavern owners (6) Hairdressers (7) Liquor salesmen (8) Taxi drivers (9) Salesmen (10) Musicians.

The same survey identified these categories as the worst tippers: (1) Senior citizens (2) People between twenty-one and twenty-four years old (3) Tourists (4) Teachers (5) Women (6) Lawyers (7) Doctors (8) Computer nerds (9) Bankers (10) Pipe smokers.

Waiters, waitresses, and bartenders identify good tippers from best to worst by what they drink in the following order: (1) Vodka (2) Rum (3) Beer (4) Tequila (5) Bourbon (6) Scotch (7) Wine (8) Gin (9) Whiskey (10) Non-alcoholic and creamy or fancy drinks with umbrellas, or frozen, layered, or flaming drinks.

How valid is the theory of six degrees of separation?

Six degrees of separation is the theory that anyone on Earth can be connected to any other person on the planet through a chain of five acquaintances. The phrase was inspired by an article in *Psychology Today* that reported a 1967 study by Stanley Milgram (1933–1984), an American social psychologist who tested the theory by having strangers randomly send packages to people several thousand miles away with only the intended recipient's name and occupation as an address. They, in turn, were instructed to pass the package on to someone they knew on a first-name basis who was most likely personally familiar with the target.

That person would do the same and so on until the package was delivered to the intended recipient. The result was that it took between five and seven intermediaries to get a package delivered.

The theory was first proposed by Hungarian writer Frigyes Karinthy (1887–1938) in a 1929 short story called "Chains." After a twenty-year study begun in 1950, mathematicians from IBM and the Massachusetts Institute of Technology were unable to confirm the theory to their own satisfaction.

In 2001, Duncan Watts of Columbia University researched the "six-degree" theory using email as the "package." When he reviewed the data collected by 48,000 senders and nineteen targets in 157 countries, Professor Watts found that the average number of intermediaries was, in fact, six.

In 1990 the American playwright John Guare had his play *Six Degrees of Separation* produced on Broadway. Starring Swoozie Kurtz and Courtenay B. Vance, it dramatized the true-life story of a young black man who conned upper-middle-class couples in Manhattan into believing he was the son of actor Sidney Poitier. The story was later turned into a movie starring Donald Sutherland and Will Smith. Around the same time a trio of college buddies, inspired by the six-degree theory, dreamed up Six Degrees of Kevin Bacon, the vastly popular trivia game.

Why do we say people showing their age are no "spring chickens"?

To say someone is "no spring chicken" is to suggest he or she is past his or her physical prime. This expression grew from a time in New England before raising chickens had become the cruelly sophisticated industry it is today. Chickens came from free-range family farms with no incubators or warm henhouses, which meant baby chicks couldn't be hatched or raised in the winter. The prime price for chickens sold during the summer was for those born the previous spring. Anything older and less succulent that was pawned off as part of the spring crop was quickly identified by shrewd shoppers as "no spring chicken," or not as young as what was being presented.

Why are homosexual men sometimes called "fags"?

"Faggot," the cruel label for homosexuals, actually began as a contemptuous slang word for a woman, especially one who was old and unpleasant. The reference was to a burden that had to be carried in the same manner as baggage and harks back to the word's original meaning.

In the thirteenth century, a faggot was a bundle of wood or twigs bound together, such as the ones carried by heretics to feed the fires that would burn them at the stake. Heretics who recanted were required to wear an embroidered figure of a faggot on their sleeves. It wasn't until 1914 that the slang word *faggot* first appeared in the United States as a reference to a male homosexual, probably derived from the earlier reference to an annoying woman. The abbreviation *fag* surfaced in 1921.

There is a misconception that male homosexuals were called faggots because they were burned at the stake, but this notion is an urban legend. Homosexuals were sometimes burned alive in Europe, but by the time England made homosexuality a capital offence in 1533, hanging was the prescribed punishment.

The Yiddish word for male homosexual is *faygele*, which literally means "little bird."

The English word *faggot* is derived from the Latin *fasces* via the French *fagot*, meaning "a bundle of wood."

Why do the Scots refer to girls as "lassies" and boys as "laddies"?

Both *lassie* and *laddie* are reminders of the Viking raids and temporary conquest of parts of Britain in the Dark and early Middle Ages. *Lass* began as the Scandinavian word *loskr* and meant someone light or slight. Around 1725 the word evolved into *lassie*, Scottish for an unmarried woman or girl. To the Vikings, *lad* was *ladde* and meant a boy or young man who was led, such as a foot soldier or a male servant. The word became *laddie* around 1546.

Extensions to pet and proper names, such as the *ie* in *laddie* or *lassie*, or the *y* in names like Robby or Donny, surfaced in Scotland around 1400 and became popularized as endearments by the poems of Robert Burns (1759–1796).

Where did the Hells Angels get their name?

The outlaw motorcycle gang known as Hells Angels grew from a small group of post–World War II servicemen who longed for the danger, excitement, and comradeship they had experienced in the wartime military. Fuelled by movies during the 1950s and media hype and their own sense of rebellion and outrageous behaviour, the Hells Angels have gone off track and grown into an international underworld organization.

The motorcycle gang took its name from a famous American B-17F bomber whose heroic crew of six named themselves and their Flying Fortress *Hell's Angels*. The aircrew, in turn, was inspired by the title of the 1930 Howard Hughes film that introduced and starred the legendary Jean Harlow.

In Fontana, California, on May 17, 1948, two small biker gangs joined to form the first Hells Angels Motorcycle Club. The initial membership was twenty-five.

The bomber crew known as Hell's Angels became famous when after flying forty-eight missions its members toured the United States, pointing out the combat scars and patches that covered their "fort." While flying a bombing run, the famous B-17's Captain Baldwin first suggested over the interphone that his men name the plane and themselves after the Hughes film. One of Baldwin's crew, remarking on the mission being flown, replied, "Why not? This is the closest to hell that angels will ever get!"

How old are baby boomers?

The baby-boom generation is different in some countries because it is defined as those children born to families of servicemen returning home after World War II and for the eighteen years following. It was decided that in North America this term included people born between 1946 and 1964. In 2006 there were about seventy-six million

BABY BOOMER BUMPER STICKERS

WHERE THERE'S A PILL THERE'S A WAY

DOWN WITH HOT PANTS

SUPPOSE THEY GAVE A WAR AND NOBODY CAME

LOVE THY NEIGHBOUR BUT DON'T GET CAUGHT

SUPPORT YOUR CHURCH — PLAY BINGO

BAN THE BOMB — SAVE THE WORLD FOR
        CONVENTIONAL WARFARE

CUSTER WORE AN ARROW SHIRT

TRUST GOD! SHE PROVIDES

IF YOU DON'T LIKE THE POLICE, NEXT TIME YOU'RE IN
        TROUBLE CALL A HIPPIE

VIETNAM — LOVE IT OR LEAVE IT

CLEAN AIR SMELLS FUNNY

LIVE DANGEROUSLY — TAKE A BREATH

HONK IF YOU LOVE JESUS

HONK IF YOU LOVE CHEESES

LADY GODIVA WAS A STREAKER

A PILL A DAY KEEPS THE STORK AWAY

EAT BEANS — AMERICA NEEDS GAS

NURSES ARE PANHANDLERS

UNEMPLOYMENT ISN'T WORKING

I OWE, I OWE, SO OFF TO WORK I GO

EX-HUSBAND IN TRUNK

MY WIFE RAN OFF WITH MY PICKUP TRUCK AND I MISS IT

GIVE ME A BREAK, I HAVE TEENAGERS

BAN BUMPER STICKERS

baby boomers in the United States and about 9.8 million in Canada. In that year the boomers began turning sixty, with the youngest, of course, being forty-two.

What dates define Generation X, Generation Y, and the Echo Boomers?

For those people born after the post–World War II baby boomers, advertisers have created labels to define their targets. Within that industry, those born between 1964 and 1983 are known as Generation X. Echo boomers, or the children of the baby boomers, were born between the late 1970s and the early 1990s. Generation Y's members are the children of Generation X and were born after 1983.

The confusion lies in the use of the word *generation* by advertisers and the media. For marketing purposes, an echo boomer can also be part of both Generations X and Y. Historically, a "generation" of humans was defined as the average interval of time between the birth of parents and their offspring — in other words, about twenty-five years.

What do European Jewish names have in common with those of Scotland?

In the sixteenth century, when surnames became necessary so that governments could enforce taxation and conscription, census-taking was introduced. This development meant that everyone needed a last name, something that was against the traditions of both the Gaels of Scotland and the Jews of Poland. Both had survived for centuries with traditional name forms such as "son of ..." (Mac or Mc in Scotland and Ben in Jewish Europe).

After Russia, Prussia, and Austria partitioned Poland in the eighteenth century, Jews, like the Scots, took the names of their hometowns or that of their noble landowners. In Prussia and Austria, the governments went one step farther and decreed that all Jewish surnames would be decided by the state.

In the first few years of the nineteenth century, E.T.A. Hoffmann (1776–1822), a Prussian administration clerk in Warsaw, Poland, amused himself by handing out insulting Jewish surnames according to his own whims, which is why so many Jewish immigrants to North America changed their names as soon as they landed.

Shmiel Gelbfisz arrived in North America from Warsaw at the turn of the twentieth century as Samuel Goldfish. He legally changed his name by keeping "Gold" and adding the last syllable of his friend Archibald Selwyn's last name. Shmiel went on to become the movie mogul Samuel Goldwyn, one of the founders of Metro-Goldwyn-Mayer or MGM.

Besides being responsible for forcing unwanted surnames on Polish Jews, E.T.A. Hoffmann was also a writer of fantasy fiction whose short story "Nutcracker and Mouse King" inspired the ballet *The Nutcracker* by Pyotr Ilyich Tchaikovsky (1840–1893).

Why is a clever child called a "whiz kid"?

Since the early twentieth century, a clever or remarkable person of any age has often been referred to as a *whiz*. The word is a shortened form of *wizard*. "Whiz kid" derives from a 1930s takeoff of the popular radio show *Quiz Kids*. A whiz in this application means anyone who has a remarkable skill.

If you're wondering why going to the bathroom is called "taking a whiz," it's because *whiz* has a cousin with another meaning. A *whizz* is a hissing sound made by an object speeding through the air.

Why is an effeminate man called a "sissy" or a "priss"?

Since 1887, when a male is unwilling or fails to meet the challenges of being a robust young man, he has sometimes been called a sissy. The word *sis* is an abbreviation of *sister*. *Sissy* was often used as an endearment for a female sibling. On the other hand, *priss* is a 1895 merger of the words *precise* or *prim* and *sis*.

Why do we call tearful, overly sentimental people "maudlin"?

A lot of drinkers are referred to as "maudlin" when they become weak and overemotional and "cry in their beer." The word is a common British alteration of Magdalene, the surname of Mary, the woman who repented and was forgiven by Jesus Christ in Luke 7:37. In medieval paintings, as a sign of repentance, Mary Magdalene is most often shown with eyes swollen from weeping. The use of her name in terms of being maudlin, meaning "tearful sentimentality," was first recorded in 1631.

ODDS & ODDITIES

The chance of giving birth to a genius is 1 in 250.

The odds of dating a supermodel are 88,000 to 1.

The odds of dating a millionaire are 215 to 1.

The odds of becoming a saint are 20,000,000 to 1.

The odds that a first marriage will survive without separation or divorce for fifteen years are 1.3 to 1.

The chance of being audited by the tax department is 1 in 100.

Why is a wise counsellor called a "mentor" or a "guru"?

The original Mentor was the name of a wise and trusted counsellor in Greek mythology who was Odysseus's friend and a trusted teacher of Telemachus, Odysseus's son. Mentor was often the goddess Athena in disguise. The word *guru* has the same meaning as *mentor* because it is the Hindi word for "honoured teacher." *Guru* was first used this way in 1966 by Canadian communications theorist Marshall McLuhan (1911–1980).

The derivative *men* in *mentor* is the same as that in *mental* and means "to think."

Why are inhabitants of the Appalachian and Ozark mountains called "hillbillies"?

The term *hillbilly* generally describes an uneducated or rough-hewn inhabitant of the Ozark and Appalachian mountains of the United States. Hillbillies are a proud culture unto themselves with amazing music that reflects their harsh, isolated existence and the origins of their forefathers. The first hillbillies were the Scots-Irish followers of Britain's King William III (1650–1702) whose Protestant Orangemen defeated the Roman Catholic allies of the former British king James II (1633–1701) at the Battle of the Boyne in Ireland in 1690. William III's followers were known as Billy Boys, and many of them immigrated to the hills of Appalachia before the American Revolution. It was during this time that British soldiers gave these people the name hillbillies, an informal reference to their previous history as supporters of King William of Orange.

In 1900 an article in the *New York Journal* described a hillbilly as a "free and untrammelled white citizen of Alabama who lives in the hills, has no means … drinks whiskey … and fires off his revolver."

In many remote Ozark areas, it is still possible to find people who speak English with a dialect that can be traced back to pre–American Revolution days.

Who were the first "rednecks"?

The concept of a redneck being a poor white farmer or labourer from the U.S. South dates back to the late 1800s, but 200 years earlier Scottish and Northern Irish Presbyterians were also known as rednecks. To show their rejection of the Church of England, they wore red cloths around their necks. The South African Boers called British soldiers rednecks for the same reason Southerners got the title. Only the fair skin of their necks was exposed to the burning sun.

SAILING
&
THE SEA

Why is someone lost in boredom said to be at "loose ends"?

The origin of this phrase is nautical and refers to the ends of the count-less number of ropes on early sailing ships. These "ends" needed to be bound tightly to prevent unravelling, which could cause disaster at sea. Whenever a captain noticed that his men had too much time on their hands, which could lead to trouble, he would order them to check the ropes and repair any "loose ends."

Why did sailors begin wearing bell-bottom trousers?

British sailors started wearing bell-bottom trousers near the end of the eighteenth century. Before then they wore "slops," a loose-fitting mid-calf-length pant. "Bells" were only worn by "swabs," or regular seamen, and not by officers. Regulation dictated that the bells be made of wide cuffs large enough to roll up to the thigh during wading or deck swabbing.

Although most eighteenth-century sailors couldn't swim, they were taught to pull up and tie the bells of their pants, creating air-filled life preservers if they fell overboard. U.S. sailors stopped wearing bell bottoms around 1998 when they became part of the dress (formal) uniform only. However, when the supply ran out in 2000, bell bottoms in the U.S. Navy disappeared altogether.

Why is a person facing serious trouble said to be in "dire straits"?

Strait is a Middle English word that was used by sailors to describe a narrow or tight and difficult-to-manoeuvre channel of water such as the Straits of Gibraltar or the Bering Strait. The word comes from the Latin *strictus*, meaning "to bind tightly." *Dire* also has a Latin root and means "terrible" or "fearsome." Although "dire straits" now signifies any serious day-to-day problem, it originally meant facing an obstacle so difficult to overcome that the odds against navigating through it successfully were overwhelming.

Why do we say that someone burdened by guilt has an "albatross" around his or her neck?

An "albatross" is a figurative stigma for shame. It refers to a guilt that never leaves you and becomes the defining characteristic of a moral burden. The albatross is a bird that symbolized good luck to sailing ships because it signalled that land was nearby. The bird's change in fortune resulted from Samuel Taylor Coleridge's 1798 poem "The Rime of the Ancient Mariner," which tells of a captain who killed an albatross after which there was a prolonged calm that stranded his ship. As a consequence, the captain was forced by the crew to wear the dead bird around his neck.

Coleridge (1772–1834) himself had his share of dire straits, battling drug addiction, marital difficulties, and personal setbacks through much of his middle years.

Why is the residue of a shipwreck called "flotsam and jetsam"?

"Flotsam and jetsam" is sometimes used broadly as "odds and ends," but its origin dates back to the late sixteenth century as a description of debris left after a shipwreck. Flotsam is whatever is left of the cargo or ship that is found floating on water. Jetsam is cargo or parts of the ship thrown overboard to lighten the ship in an emergency and which subsequently sinks or is washed ashore. Today the expression might also be used to describe debris from a plane wreck.

Flotsam came to English through the Old French verb *floter,* meaning "to float." *Jetsam* is an alteration of *jettison.*

Valuable items thrown into the sea but attached to a buoy so they can be recovered after the ship goes down are called "lagan."

What is the meaning of the nautical phrase "before the mast"?

In his book *Two Years Before the Mast,* the American lawyer and author Richard Henry Dana (1815–1882) reveals his experiences as a young man at sea aboard the brig *Pilgrim* in 1834. The mast of a sailing ship was the boundary between the quarters of officers in the rear and the crew in front. Dana kept a diary of the wretched treatment and conditions experienced by a common seaman living "before the mast," and from his notes he compiled his book, published in 1840.

Why do we say that somebody who is being treated badly has been "hung out to dry"?

Discipline on early British sailing ships was necessary but often extreme. The lash or cat-o'-nine-tails left sailors scarred for life, but the act of keel hauling — tying a victim with rope and pulling him under the ship, sometimes more than once — was the discipline feared most. If the prisoner survived drowning, he was suspended from the yardarm where he was left hanging or "hung out to dry" for a predetermined period of time, then cut down to contemplate his misdemeanours.

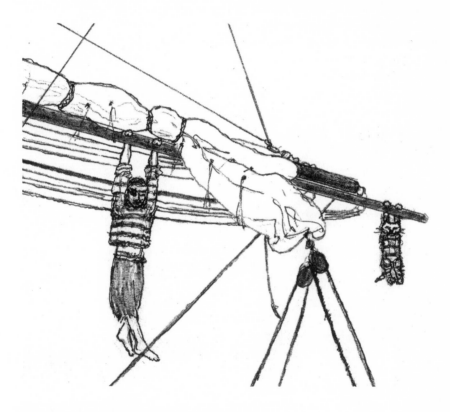

Why were sailors so superstitious?

Life-and-death situations always give rise to superstitions, so early sailors took no chances and followed many good-luck rituals beyond prayer. One such ritual was to raise or "step" the main mast on a silver coin from the year a ship was built to keep the wind "happy." As a backup, horseshoes were nailed to the mast to keep storms at bay.

Sighting a dolphin brought good luck, but killing them could be disastrous. Killing a gull was unforgivable, since it was believed that these birds carried the souls of sailors lost at sea.

Why do sailors sing "shanties"?

Sea shanties are the songs sung by sailors working on the great sailing ships of a more romantic time. A shanty man leads the songs. He chants a line, and the sailors respond within the rhythm of their work. Shanties take different forms, depending on the labour being done. There are short-haul shanties and long-haul shanties for operating the sails. There are shanties used to raise and lower the anchor, and there are shanties whalers used to sing.

Around 1867, sea songs or "chanties" became known as shanties, from the French *chantez*, meaning "to sing." The word *shanty*, "a small, crude cabin," is French Canadian and has a different root. The term *shanty town* was first recorded in Canada in 1876. The designation Shanty Irish was inspired by the title of a 1928 book by hard-boiled American writer Jim Tully (1886–1947).

What makes a ship a "tramp steamer"?

Today a "tramp steamer" is more accurately described as a "tramp freighter," since steam engines have long been replaced by diesels. In either case, just like human "tramps" who wander the streets, these ships navigate the oceans of the world without a fixed schedule, looking for ports of call that will offer the best price for their cargoes.

Tramp steamers were often the way adventurous people got to exotic places during the first half of the twentieth century. A number of famous writers, American playwright Eugene O'Neill (1888–1953) and British novelist Malcolm Lowry (1909–1957) to name two, shipped aboard tramp freighters when they were young and later wrote about their experiences.

How do large ships anchor in deep water?

Because of the oceans' depth, a harbour anchor is of no use to a ship at sea. In its simplest form, a sea anchor is a canvas sack attached to a metal ring. Tying it to the stern of a boat and dragging it through the water creates resistance, which slows the boat down. In a strong gale, sea anchors can make the difference between life and death.

QUICKIES

Did You Know ...

that blue blazers originated as military jackets worn by British sailors on the nineteenth-century ship HMS *Blazer*?

Why do sailors call the bottom of the sea "Davy Jones's locker"?

"Davy Jones" seems like such a nice normal name, but this mythical creature struck terror into the hearts of ancient mariners. Going to his locker meant you were a man overboard and destined to die because the locker was at the bottom of the sea where biblical images of Jonah and the whale came into play. Davy Jones presided over all evil spirits in the sea and could shape-shift into hideous forms, often perching on the riggings during hurricanes or shipwrecks.

Davy Jones first appeared in literature in 1751 in *The Adventures of Peregrine Pickle* by British novelist Tobias Smollett.

There is a colourful legend that Davy Jones was a pub owner who would get young men drunk and then confine them in a "locker" where he stored his beer until he could sell them to a ship short of hands.

What is the origin of the word *squeegee?*

A squeegee brings to mind either spring cleaning or an annoying panhandler at a traffic light. The word probably had an equally unpleasant effect on the sailors who gave the scraping instrument its name. *Squeege* was an eighteenth-century alteration of *squeeze* or *press* and was the inspiration for the name of a tool used for scraping the decks of ships. In *Moby Dick*, American author Herman Melville (1819–1891) called the tool a "squilgee," but other sources indicate that *squeegee* was a nautical term for the instrument as early as 1844.

Why does "careen" describe dangerous driving?

We describe a "careening" car as one that lurches or swerves from side to side in a dangerous manner, because the word *careen* is the nautical term for *keel*. Sailing ships leaning precariously while sailing into the wind must careen or steer from side to side. These ships needed to have their bottoms repaired regularly and scraped to rid them of barnacles. When no dry dock was available, the captain would find a suitable beach, then run his ship aground at low tide. The vessel was then "careened" or tipped over, exposing the keel and allowing sailors to clean and restore one side of the hull. Once both sides were finished, and the tide returned, the ship would float off the beach and sail back to sea.

Why are windows in ships and planes called "portholes"?

Openings on the sides of a ship have been called portholes since 1243. The word *port* comes from the Latin *porta*, which means "door" or "gate." Because steering apparatus or the "steerboard" was on the right, ships of the time docked on their left, which was originally known as the "larboard" side because it's the loading side. In the sixteenth century, "larboard" gave way to "portside" to avoid confusion with the similar-sounding "starboard" or right side. Portholes are most commonly used to describe windows on both sides of airplanes and ships, but the term comes from the openings on the portside to load cargo onto ancient ships.

When is a flag flown upside down a signal of distress?

The use of flags to signal distress is a very old naval tradition, but flying the national flag upside down isn't one of them. From a distance it's hard to read whether a flag is or isn't upside down. The rule was that when you needed help, you drew attention to your ship by doing something unusual such as arranging the sails in an un-seaman-like manner or by flying the ensign upright but in an unusual place. The most commonly agreed-upon distress signal in Britain's Royal Navy was to tie an ensign into a "wheft" or a "knot" and fly it from the foretop-gallant masthead. The word *wheft* is a variant of *waif*, which literally means "unclaimed property."

An ensign is a national flag displayed on ships and aircraft, while an insignia is a badge or emblem indicating rank, unit membership, or nationality. A flag is a cloth ensign and derives from *flagstone* because it is square and flat. On land an ensign tied in a wheft and flown upside down over a fort was sometimes a signal of distress, but the knot was still the key. Today there are sixteen standardized international naval distress signals.

Why is someone standing apart said to be "aloof"?

If someone is emotionally or physically reserved, we say they are "aloof." This remoteness is sometimes interpreted as being regally snobbish or simply shy. *Aloof* is derived from the nautical word *loof*, which in early sixteenth-century English meant "windward direction" or "the weather side of the ship." The helmsman directed the ship into the wind to keep from being blown onto coastal rocks. He was ordered to keep his distance from the shore with the order "Hold a-loof," which is how *aloof* took on the general meaning of "keeping clear."

Why is a gentle wind called a "breeze"?

In 1626 in a guide for young seamen, the English captain and explorer John Smith (1580–1631) recorded the first use of the word *breeze* in a list of winds in order of their severity. These included a calm, a breeze, a gale, a gust, a storm, a spout, a tornado, a monsoon, and a hurricane. Captain Smith spelled *breeze* as *brese* and had taken it from the Spanish word *briza*, meaning a light wind.

HEALTH

Why do we say that someone in good physical condition is as "fit as a fiddle"?

If you are "fit as a fiddle," you are in great shape. When the early North American settlers gathered for a barn dance, it was often an all-night session of dancing and romancing for the hard-working and socially starved farmers. The local band of amateurs was led by the fiddler who needed great endurance and stamina to play until the cows came home. This gave us the expression "fit as a fiddler," which evolved into "fit as a fiddle."

How do we avoid trouble by keeping "danger at bay"?

Keeping danger at bay obviously means to take action to protect your interests, but how does *bay* figure into it? The ancients believed the bay tree had mystical powers because it seemed never to be struck by lightning. The Greeks and Romans wore its leaves during thunderstorms as protection, and wreaths were made from bay leaves to symbolize invincibility for athletes and victory for warriors. During epidemics and

ODDS & ODDITIES

The chance of drowning in one's bathtub is 1 in 685,000. A person is more than twice as likely to drown in a swimming pool than in a lake, ocean, or river. The odds against fatally slipping during a bath or shower are 2,232 to 1.

The chance of being struck by lightning in the course of a year is 1 in 240,000, while in one's lifetime it is 1 in 3,000. The odds against being killed by lightning are 2,320,000 to 1.

The odds against dying from an insect, snake, or spider bite are 100,000 to 1.

The chance of dying from choking on food is 1 in 370,035. The chance of dying from food poisoning is 1 in 3,000,000.

The chance of dying from a shark attack is 1 in 300,000,000.

plagues such as the bubonic horror in London, many people carried bay leaves, hoping to keep the sickness "at bay."

What causes "goose bumps" on our skin when we are frightened?

Fear not only causes goose bumps, but it also makes our hair stand on end, and both reactions are related. When we are frightened, our bodies draw blood away from our extremities (like skin) and redirect it to support our vital organs. As a defence against this tendency, our very hairy primitive ancestors developed an evolutionary response to keep the body warm. When blood is drawn away from the skin, it triggers tiny muscles that tighten the skin and force body hair to stand up to trap heat. This reaction causes stiffening where we once had a lot more body hair, and because the raised flesh looks like the skin of a plucked goose, we call the result goose bumps.

Why is rabies sometimes called "hydrophobia"?

It was once believed that dogs with rabies were afraid of water, which isn't the case, but in Greek, *phobia* means "fear" and *hydro* is "water," which is why the disease was called hydrophobia. To be made raving mad from rabies surfaced in 1804 as *rabid*. It's from the Latin word *rabere* — "to be raving mad."

In the Welsh and Breton languages, the belief that the relationship between dogs and the rage of rabies and hydrophobia was so strong that their words for hydrophobia are compounds based on their words for *dog*, which in Welsh is *cynddaredd*, and in Breton, *kounnar*. *Enrage*, on the other hand, is Old French for "to be made rabid."

Why is the vehicle that takes people to the hospital called an "ambulance"?

The French began treating wounded soldiers in the field in 1809 by bringing the hospital to the injured. Those who could walk or be carried on a stretcher were taken to a tent or field hospital and treated immediately. The French verb for *to walk* is *ambulare*, which gave us the English word *amble*. In 1242 the word *hospital*, like *hospitality*, first took the meaning of "a shelter for the needy" and began referring to an "institution for sick people" in 1549. So the literal translation of *ambulance* is "a place to which the needy can walk or be carried." During the Crimean War in the mid-nineteenth century, the term *ambulance* was transferred to horse-drawn vehicles that for the first time conveyed the wounded from the field to the hospital.

Canada's first hospital was a "sick bay" at Port Royal in Acadia between 1606 and 1613. It was run by two male attendants from the Order of St. Jean de Dieu.

Canadian doctor Norman Bethune (1890–1939) introduced delivering blood to the battlefield using a battered old station wagon during the Spanish Civil War in 1936 and then later improved his battlefield ambulance service while in China, where he died himself from septicemia contracted during the course of his work as a surgeon.

QUICKIES

Did You Know ...

that on the human hand the middle finger is exactly as long as the hand is wide?

that of the 206 bones in the human body, one-quarter of them are in the feet?

How did Queen Victoria revolutionize childbirth?

Britain's Queen Victoria (1819–1901) was very familiar with the discomforts of childbirth. During delivery of the first seven of her nine children, Her Majesty suffered a lot of pain. This agony made her very interested in the discovery of chloroform, which became available as an anesthetic early in her reign. Despite protests against the practice from the Church of England and the medical establishment, she allowed her doctor to administer chloroform during the delivery of her eighth child, Prince Leopold, in 1853. The success of that delivery led to anesthetics quickly gaining popularity among England's influential upper classes.

The queen was so impressed with the benefits of chloroform that she knighted one of her physicians, Dr. James Simpson (1811–1870), who was the first to use it as an anesthetic in 1847.

How are "burn degrees" assessed?

The seriousness of a burn is assessed in degrees depending on the number of layers of skin involved. A sunburn, or a red mark on a finger touched to an iron, is a first-degree burn. A second-degree burn blisters. Third-degree burns mean that all skin is destroyed right down to the layer of tissue under the skin. Burns on faces, hands, and feet can be more serious than a wound on the thigh, for example, because of the importance of these body parts. Burns to the genital area are also more dangerous because they are vulnerable to infection.

Second- and third-degree burns always require immediate medical attention (the first thirty seconds are crucial) to remove the cause of the burn, cool the skin, and protect against infection.

ODDS & ODDITIES

The chance of having a stroke is 1 in 6. The chance of dying from heart disease is 1 in 3. The chance of getting arthritis is 1 in 7. The chance of getting the flu in the course of a year is 1 in 10. The chance of contracting the human version of mad cow disease is 1 in 40,000,000. The chance of dying from any kind of fall is 1 in 20,666.

What are "patent medicines"?

All new inventions, including medicines, require a patent; that is, their components must be revealed. The word *patent* means an "open letter" and is a grant made by a government that confers upon the creator of an invention the sole right to make, use, and sell that invention for a set period of time. During the nineteenth and early twentieth centuries, travelling medicine shows sold what they called "patent" concoctions, claiming cures for all manner of illnesses. They got around the open-letter concept of a patent and kept their ingredients secret by taking a patent out on the shape of the bottle or its label instead of the formula inside. The patent medicine industry began a slow decline in 1906 after years of critical newspaper articles led to the passage of the U.S. Pure Food and Drug Act, which required ingredients to be listed on labels.

Patent is from the Latin *patentum*, meaning "lying open." Many brand names that started as patent medicines are still with us, including Absorbine Jr., Bromo-Seltzer, Pepsi-Cola, and Coca-Cola.

Why is an unstable person called a "crackpot"?

A crackpot is an irrational person. Crackpots have always been with us, but the word only came into use in the late 1800s. The term plays on the obsolete use of the word *pot* to describe a skull. It suggests that the person in question has a cracked skull, which is causing him or her to behave in a mad, foolish, or eccentric manner.

TRAVEL

Why are traffic lights red, green, and yellow?

Red, green, and yellow traffic lights developed directly from the trial and error of controlling railways during the nineteenth century. Trains needed advance warning to prevent fatal accidents and collisions. The first choice was red for stop, which was logical because red had symbolized danger for thousands of years. During the 1830s, engineers tried using green for caution and clear for go, but sunlight reflecting off clear lights gave false signals. So engineers solved the problem by introducing yellow for caution and making green stand for go. The very first traffic light using this system was introduced in Cleveland, Ohio, in 1914.

What city first used stop signs?

Stop signs first showed up in Detroit, Michigan, in 1915. They were black on white and smaller than modern signs. Until then traffic-control devices were generally manual, using semaphores (flags), policemen in traffic towers, and hand-turned stop-and-go signs. In the 1920s, black-on-yellow signs were introduced, while white-on-red signs appeared in 1954.

Mounting height has also evolved. Early signs were about three feet off the ground. Modern signs are more than six feet high.

What does "MG" stand for on the classic British sports car?

The MGB is the best-known classic British sports car and was introduced in 1962 as an update of the original MGA, which first appeared in 1955. There were approximately 375,000 MGBs built before the company went out of business in 1981. The MG stands for Morris Garages, a retail outlet that was established in 1911 and that began selling MG-badged Morris Specials in the 1920s.

Why is the last car on a freight rain called a "caboose"?

Up until the 1980s, laws required freight trains to have a caboose. It was a little shack on wheels and served as an office, a kitchen, and a bedroom for the crew. The caboose was also an observation deck from which brakemen could watch the train for shifting loads, overheating wheels, and other problems. The first such shanties were set up as tents on flatcars as early as 1830. *Caboose* is from an ancient German sailing term, *kabhuse*, a temporary kitchen set up on the deck of a ship. Some of the nicknames used by rail crews for the caboose were "clown wagon," "hack," "brain-box," and "palace."

Why is a carrying bag called a "tote bag"?

During the seventeenth century, American slaves did most of the heavy lifting in the U.S. South. Most of these slaves were from West Africa and still spoke their native Bantu languages. *Tota* is the Bantu

ODDS & ODDITIES

The odds of being killed during the course of a year in any sort of transportation accident are 77 to 1.

The chance that one's next car ride will be one's last is 1 in 4,000,000, while the odds of being killed on a five-mile bus trip are 500,000,000 to 1. The odds of being killed while riding a horse are six times greater than the odds of meeting one's demise on a bus trip.

The chance of dying from a car accident during one's lifetime is 1 in 18,585. Walking is safer. The one-year chance of dying while a pedestrian is about 1 in 50,000.

The chance of dying in an airplane accident is 1 in 354,319.

The odds of being killed in any sort of non-transportation accident are 69 to 1.

The chance of being killed in a terrorist attack while visiting a foreign country is 1 in 650,000.

The chance of dying from parts falling off an airplane is 1 in 10,000,000.

word for "lifting" or "carrying." From these slaves and then through the plantation owners, *tota* entered English as *tote*. The term *tote bag* was derived from *tote* and popularized around 1900.

Why do we say we're "stumped" if we can't proceed?

We have all been stumped at one time or another, whether by a private or professional circumstance or perhaps by a mathematical or legal problem. *Stumped*, as in unable to proceed, comes from the first crude highways built by the early settlers in North America. It was the law that when trees were felled the stumps had to be at least fifteen inches high. That was fine until it rained and the ground turned muddy. The wheels on the wagons using the road would often sink until the axles got caught on tree stumps. The wagons couldn't move forward because they had been "stumped."

Why is something incredibly impressive called a "real doozy"?

A "real doozy" may be an old-fashioned expression, but it still means something remarkable. It was used to describe one of the most impressive cars ever made. Built between 1920 and 1937, the Duesenberg was the best and most expensive American car ever built. During the Great Depression, and at a time when a Ford sold for $500, a top-of-the-line Doozy retailed for $25,000. With a custom-built body and a high-horsepower engine, the Duesenberg quickly became a favourite vehicle of the rich and famous. It still is! As one of the most collectible cars in the world, Duesenbergs in mint condition have sold for millions of dollars. Now that's a doozy!

What happened to the "station wagon"?

A station wagon was originally a horse-drawn carriage. The name transferred to cars in 1904, and in 1929 the first modern station wagon was manufactured. It referred to a car big enough to haul people and luggage to and from railway stations. Prior to the 1930s, most automobile makers used hardwoods to frame the passenger compartments of their vehicles, but when steel took over, designers extended a wood-panel finish to the exterior of multipurpose passenger-and-cargo cars.

These became the classic station wagons that grew in popularity with suburban families after World War II. Station wagons were largely replaced by minivans or sport-utility vehicles (SUVs) during the 1980s and 1990s and have all but disappeared from the world's roads.

Where did the Rolls-Royce automobile get its name?

Charles Rolls (1877–1910), a salesman, and Henry Royce (1863–1933), an electrical engineer, got together in 1906 to produce a car that would be sold exclusively by Rolls. They agreed the car would be called a Rolls-Royce. The first model was the Silver Ghost, which they produced until 1925. The company continued in private owner-ship until 1971 when financial problems in its aircraft division led to a takeover by the British government. Today Rolls-Royce is owned by the German automobile maker Bayerische Motoren Werke (BMW).

Rolls-Royce is highly regarded for its engines. They powered many of the Spitfires and Hurricanes used in the Battle of Britain during World War II.

Why is "thumbing a ride" called "hitchhiking"?

Hitchhiking is a combination of two words. The term has two origins that collided in 1923 as an inexpensive way of travelling. *Hiking* means to "walk vigorously" and has been around forever. In 1578 the word *hitch* surfaced as a nautical description of "fastening with a hook" but eventually gained broader use as in "hitching a team of horses to a wagon" or "hitching a trailer to a car." *Hitchhike* was first employed in 1880 to describe hitching a sled to a moving car. The use of the thumb by someone looking for a ride is a symbolic "hook" to signal the hitch-hiker's wish to become attached to a passing car.

FOOD
&
DRINK

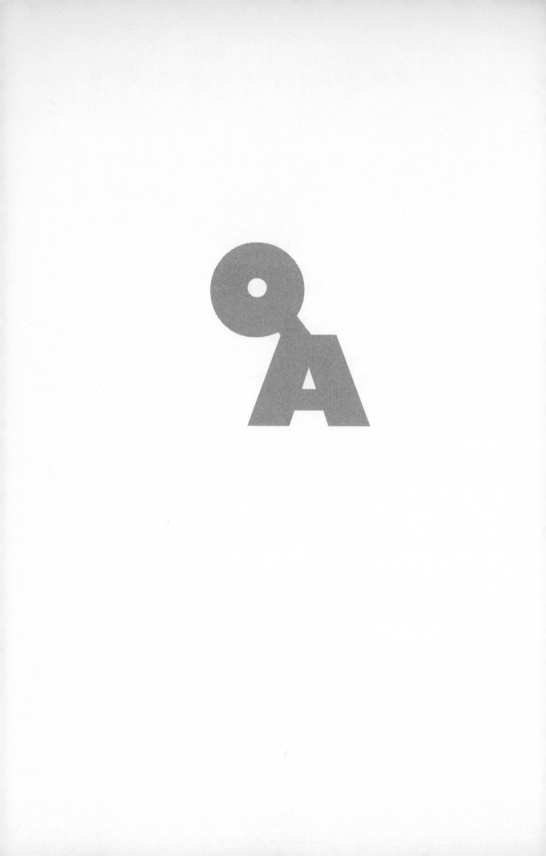

Why is a certain kind of bread roll called a "bagel"?

Many North Americans associate bagels with breakfast, but few people realize they were originally a homage to a Polish king who saved Vienna, Austria, from a Turkish invasion in 1683. A local Jewish baker thanked the king by creating a special hard roll in the shape of a stirrup to commemorate the Polish cavalry. One word used to describe a stirrup in Austria is *beugel*.

In Yiddish, *bagel* means a "ring," often a bracelet. Sprinkled with onions, a bagel is called a *bialy*, for the Polish city Bialystock.

Why is chocolate-flavoured coffee called "mocha"?

Mocha coffee got its name around 1773 when Ethiopian beans shipped from the Yemeni port city of Mocha became the most popular coffee in Europe. In the mid-nineteenth century, Americans began adding chocolate to mocha coffee as a flavouring, but it wasn't until recently when boutique coffee shops coined the term that mocha coffee took on the meaning of "chocolate-flavoured." Mocha coffee's primary definition is still officially "a pungent, rich Arabian coffee."

Who invented the Caesar salad?

In the beginning, a Caesar salad was made with whole leaves of romaine lettuce, tossed at the table, and eaten with the fingers. It was intended as an entrée. Today, served at restaurants of every type, it is a salad of convenience and often includes chicken or beef. When the salad was first introduced, though, the non-vegetable ingredients were strictly seafood such as anchovies and shrimp. The salad was created in 1924 by Caesar Cardini (1896–1956) at his Italian restaurant in Tijuana, Mexico.

Why do we say that someone well off is living "high on the hog"?

"High on the hog" is a recent expression that dates back only to the mid-1940s. It means you can afford to eat well. The best pork cuts (chops, hams, roasts, et cetera) are found higher on the pig than those traditionally prepared and eaten by the less affluent. Of course, being poor doesn't mean you can't eat well. Delicious meals have been made from those areas "low on the hog" (feet, belly, knuckles, and jowls). These meals were eaten by fieldhands and hard labourers who had worked up a hearty appetite, so being hungry might have made these dishes even more enjoyable to them than those eaten by the overfed upper classes.

Why is a party bowl of mixed drinks called "punch"?

Punch is usually a mixture of fruit and soda drinks combined with alcohol and served at large gatherings. It originated from the British colonization of northern India after the colonizers discovered a refreshing native drink made from five ingredients: rice alcohol blended with tea, sugar, and lemon, then diluted with water. The Hindi word for *five* (the number of ingredients) is *punch*.

Why are sausages and mashed potatoes called "bangers and mashed"?

"Bangers and mashed"' is a traditional English meal of sausages, mashed potatoes, gravy, and very often pork and beans. Nothing could be more working-class or middle-class comforting than this dish. *Banger*, as slang for *sausage*, dates from 1919 and refers to the noise made when the skin of a frying sausage explodes in the pan. It literally "bangs."

Why was a prospector's credit line called a "grub stake"?

The first thing most poor gold prospectors needed to keep going was food and supplies. They would make a deal to share their future success with a general store or a wealthy acquaintance in exchange for credit to buy food, shovels, picks, and a pan to sift the gravel of a stream for nuggets. This credit was called a "grub stake." *Grub*, in this case, is a reference to shallow digging, as in "grubbing around." *Grub* can also mean "food."

Why is a long drinking spree called a "bender"?

A "bender" is a prolonged, irresponsible, and dangerous bout of drinking and took its name from the patrons of London, England, alehouses

QUICKIES

Did You Know ...

that *chowder* derives from the French Canadian settler's word *chaudière*, a catch-all cooking pot for stews and soups made from whatever was at hand?

that *potato* comes from the Haitian aboriginal word *batata* through the Spanish *patata* for sweet potato?

that Daiquiri is the name of a village in eastern Cuba?

that tequila is a liquor named after a town in west-central Mexico?

that the word *rum* is an abbreviation of *rumbullion*?

that *whiskey*, as a word, comes from Gaelic and literally means "water of life"?

that the word *aquavit* is derived from the Latin *aqua vitae* and also means "water of life"?

that the word *vodka* in Russian literally means "little water"?

that the word *gin* is a shortened form of the Swiss city Geneva, which in Middle Dutch is *Geniver*, which is also a name for the juniper tree that grows the berries that give the liquor gin its flavour?

that the word *lager* in German means "storehouse," therefore *lager beer* means "beer brewed for keeping"?

during the 1850s. To promote drinking, it was common for a tavern to offer patrons all they could drink for a tuppence a day, so sixpence was good for three days. The sixpence coin, which was worth about a quarter, was nicknamed a "bender" because if it wasn't phony it could be easily bent. Since this bendable coin guaranteed three days of libation, the subsequent binge became known as a "bender."

How did "allspice" get its name?

Allspice is not a combination of spices; it is one spice with a flavour that hints at several others. Europeans discovered allspice in Jamaica where, because its berry looks like a peppercorn, it is called Jamaica pepper. The other spices its flavour emulates are cinnamon, cloves, and nutmeg.

Who invented Smarties?

Smarties are a British invention. In 1937, Rowntree of the United Kingdom introduced a line of chocolate beans that, a year later, were given the name Smarties. Packaged in cylindrical tubes, the original eight colours were red, yellow, orange, green, mauve, pink, light brown (coffee centre), and brown (chocolate centre). In 1989 the brown was replaced by blue.

Rowntree merged with the British candy-maker Mackintosh in 1969, and in 1988 the Swiss food-and-beverage conglomerate Nestlé took over Rowntree Mackintosh.

Nearly 16,000 Smarties are eaten every minute in the United Kingdom. Each day about 570,000 tubes of Smarties are made at Nestlé's York factory and shipped to the Middle East, Far East, and South America.

Smarties are also manufactured in Canada by Nestlé, but are not available in the United States because another candy producer has trademarked that name.

How did Pepsi-Cola get its name?

During the 1890s, Caleb Bradham (1867–1934), a pharmacist in New Bern, North Carolina, invented a drink for sale to his customers. At first it was only available at his store, so people called it Brad's Drink. Bradham preferred to call it Pepsi-Cola because he claimed it aided digestion by relieving dyspepsia, a gastric problem, and it tasted a lot like a more established product named Coca-Cola. In 1902, Bradham patented the drink, and his company was successful until 1923 when the high price of sugar forced him into bankruptcy. The company started up again shortly afterwards under new owners. However, Bradham never got back into the business. He died in 1934, owning less capital than he had when he started Pepsi.

Some people argue that pepsin, an enzyme good for treating stomach upset, not dyspepsia, was the source of Pepsi's name, but others say pepsin wasn't part of the original recipe.

Cola comes from the West African Mandingo word kolo, a type of tree that grows the leaves that provide a key ingredient for Pepsi-Cola and Coca-Cola.

Where does the expression "bumper crop" come from?

A "bumper crop" is a result of extraordinary abundance. You can have a bumper business, bumper crowds, or bumper crops. This ancient use of bumper comes from a drinking goblet called a "bumper," which was filled to the brim when used for toasts. While quaffing a bumper of ale, drinkers touched (or bumped) these goblets against one another during a festive or celebratory occasion such as an excellent harvest, business growth, or full houses at theatrical performances.

How were "licorice allsorts" invented?

Licorice has been popular in Britain since the Middle Ages when the Crusaders returned with the plant it is made from. Many different candies have evolved that contain licorice, including varieties that surround or layer the licorice with coconut paste. In 1899 a sales representative named Charlie Thompson for the Bassett Company accidentally dropped a tray holding samples of licorice candies in front of a customer. As Thompson picked them up off the floor, the customer asked if he could order them all as a mixture, and "licorice allsorts" were born.

Why is an easy task called a "piece of cake"?

Nothing could be more immediately rewarding than a piece of cake, and to indicate delight, we sometimes say a chore was a "piece of cake." The expression first appears in English literature in a 1936 Ogden Nash (1902–1971) poem called "Primrose Path." During World War II, the

phrase was adopted by British pilots to describe a target that was easy and fun to attack or destroy, and from there the expression graduated into everyday English.

What is "Yorkshire pudding"?

The eating customs of the poor from all over the world were intended to fill stomachs with little cost. Yorkshire pudding is one of England's answers to this culinary problem. Although we think of pudding as a dessert, Yorkshire pudding is quite different. It can be eaten as a dessert with the addition of toppings, but it is a savoury dish that really shines when it is eaten with meat. The recipe is similar to pancakes, but the batter is cooked in an oven. Traditionally, the batter would be showered with the drippings of a leg of mutton. Today it is more often cooked with the fat from roast beef. Cooked properly, it rises in airy majesty out of its pan and spills over the sides.

A popular variation on Yorkshire pudding is toad in the hole, which is made by roasting sausages in the Yorkshire pudding batter.

Known as "drippings pudding" since the Middle Ages, Yorkshire pudding got its current name from Hannah Glasse, an eighteenth-century cook from northern England who included the formula in a popular book of recipes.

Why do we look wistfully back upon our "salad days"?

Salad days are the "green" days of our youth. William Shakespeare refers to "salad days" negatively when he has Cleopatra mention them in his play *Antony and Cleopatra*, where she claims that her youthful naïveté led to her love affair with Julius Caesar. Since then the phrase has come to mean "youthful good times that are fondly remembered." Curiously, the word *salad* comes from a Latin word meaning "salted vegetables."

Why is a dried grape called a "raisin"?

A raisin is, of course, a dried grape, and like two-thirds of the English language, the word *raisin* comes from Old French, where it means "grape," shrivelled or otherwise. The word *grape* also comes from Old French and means "bunch of grapes." Sultanas and Thompson seedless grapes are the two varieties commonly enlisted to make raisins. Sultanas are used to create golden raisins, while Thompsons fashion dark ones, or they are lightened with sulfur dioxide to turn them golden.

A raisin is a "worried" grape.

Why is a type of beer called "India pale ale"?

India pale ale dates from the late eighteenth century and was developed by the Hodgson's Company to solve the problem of getting fresh-tasting beer to soldiers and sailors in India and other British colonies in sailing ships that had to navigate hot, tropical waters. Unlike most British beers of the time, India pale ale had a very high hop and alcohol content, which countered bacteria that made beer taste sour. The original India pale ale was copper-coloured. It was called pale because it was lighter than brown, porter, or stout ales. The servicemen appreciated no longer having to drink "skunky" beer.

What is the difference between brandy and cognac?

There is no difference in formula. Brandy is an abbreviation of brandy-wine and is any spirit distilled from either wine or fermented fruit juice. Cognac is also a brandy but is so called because it is exclusive to the Cognac region of France. The word *brandywine* comes from the Dutch *brandewijn*, which means "burnt wine," because the drink is distilled. All brandywine or brandy is "burnt" or "distilled wine."

Some types of brandies are: ouzo, flavoured with anise and originating in Greece; grappa, distilled from the crushed residue from wine-making and originating in Italy; kirsch, distilled from cherries and originating in Germany; slivovitz, produced from crushed plums and originating in the Balkans; and calvados, created from fermented apple cider and originating in France.

CUSTOMS

Why is a husband-to-be called a "groom"?

Bride comes from the Old English word *bryd*, while at the same time the word *guma* simply meant "a young man." The two together, *brydguma*, referred to a suitor looking for a wife. This compound changed in the sixteenth century when *groom* evolved within folk language to take over from *guma* as a description of a young man, boy, or lad who was commonly hired to work the stables and groom horses among other chores but who was still seeking a wife.

How important is the colour in a gift of flowers?

Throughout time flowers sent as gifts have had unspoken meanings and are steeped in centuries of tradition. For example, red flowers represent love, respect, passion, and courage. Pink flowers express perfect happiness, grace, thankfulness, and admiration and are an appeal for trust. Yellow flowers mean friendship, joy, jealousy, and an appeal for affection. White flowers signify innocence, purity, secrecy, or silence, while those that are peach or coral send a message of enthusiasm, desire, joyful modesty, and shyness. Purple is a declaration of passionate hope and fidelity.

Different kinds of flowers also send the recipient a personal message. Roses say "know that I love you." Carnations affirm "you are beautiful and I am proud of you." Daffodils insist "you are a brave and good person." Chrysanthemums proclaim "I am faithful to you." Gladioli admit "I admire your character." Irises inform "I send my compliments and congratulations." Orchids declare "you are in my heart." Snapdragons reveal "I desire you." Sunflowers broadcast "my thoughts are pure." Tulips announce "I am declaring that I love you."

Who started the custom of giving a dozen roses to a lover?

It was the Persians (Iranians) who initiated the idea of communicating through flowers, and the custom was introduced to Europe courtesy of Sweden's King Charles XII (1682–1718), who lived as an exile in Turkey in the early eighteenth century. In Persia every flower had a meaning. This notion captured the hearts of Europeans, who began carrying out complete conversations by exchanging different kinds of flowers. In the language of flowers, roses are said to communicate love and passion, so a dozen is like shouting out loud!

As important as roses are to Valentine's Day, the real flower of the day ought to be a violet. Legend says that violets grew outside the window area of the prison cell occupied by St. Valentine prior to his martyrdom in 269 AD. It was said that he crushed up the petals of the violets to make ink for writing letters.

Why do humans kiss?

The average person spends two weeks kissing during his or her full lifetime. The romantic or erotic kiss is a sensual genetic memory search for compatibility, whether on the lips or elsewhere, and is revealed to the brain through smell and taste. Kissing originated from prehistoric mothers breast-feeding, then chewing and pushing food into their infants' mouths with their tongues. Sigmund Freud (1856–1939) described the kiss as "an unconscious repetition of infantile delight in feeding."

Smell is the primary ingredient of the kissing ritual for some cultures such as the Inuit (Eskimos), who believe that exhaled breath reveals a person's soul. Exchanging breath in this sense is a spiritual union. This concept has a parallel in Christian dogma (Genesis 2:7), which reveals that God infused the spirit of life into his creatures by breathing into them.

Hygiene has a lot to do with the success of a romantic kiss. In medieval England, it was common during a town fair for a young woman to pick an apple and fill it with cloves. She would then approach a man she had chosen for romance and offer him the apple. After he ate it, the man would have his breath sweetened by the cloves, making a kiss from him at least palatable.

Of the many different kinds of kisses (for friends, family, or babies), one of the most interesting is the ceremonial kiss. This type is common in European countries or high society where state dignitaries offer each other a quick kiss on each side of the face. This custom isn't simply good manners; it's an ancient political gesture symbolizing goodwill between different peoples or tribes.

Finally, there is the Mafia kiss of death, which was inspired by the New Testament and is related to the kiss Judas gave to Jesus Christ when he betrayed him to the authorities.

Why do the British excuse bad language with "pardon my French"?

To the English, "pardon my French" usually means "you can put it where the sun doesn't shine." It's a non-apologetic apology. The expression is as old as the historic wars waged between France and Britain, and we can be certain the French have similar expressions about the English. Hatred aroused during war frequently leads to bigotry that instills a necessary passion within those who do the killing.

There are dozens of English expressions defaming the Dutch and Scots for the same reason. To say "pardon my French" means "I'm about to say something vulgar … like something you would expect from a Frenchman."

Examples of French customs that the British found revolting are: French kissing (kissing with the tongue) and French lessons (a euphemism for prostitution — oral sex).

What are the traditional and modern anniversary gifts?

Anniversary	Traditional	Modern
First	Paper	Clocks
Second	Cotton	China
Third	Leather or Crystal	Glass
Fourth	Fruit or Flowers	Appliances
Fifth	Wood	Silverware
Sixth	Candy	Iron Wood
Seventh	Wool or Copper	Desk Sets
Eighth	Bronze or Pottery	Linens or Lace
Ninth	Pottery	Leather
Tenth	Tin or Aluminum	Diamond Jewellery
Eleventh	Steel	Fashion Jewellery
Twelfth	Silk or Linen	Pearls
Thirteenth	Lace or Textiles	Furs
Fourteenth	Ivory or Gold	Jewelry
Fifteenth	Crystal	Watches

Anniversary	Traditional	Modern
Twentieth	China	Platinum
Twenty-Fifth	Silver	Silver
Thirtieth	Pearl	Diamond
Thirty-Fifth	Coral	Jade
Fortieth	Ruby	Ruby
Forty-Fifth	Sapphire	Sapphire
Fiftieth	Gold	Gold
Fifty-Fifth	Emerald	Emerald
Sixtieth	Diamond	Diamond

Diamonds are appropriate from this point on.

HISTORY
&
POLITICS

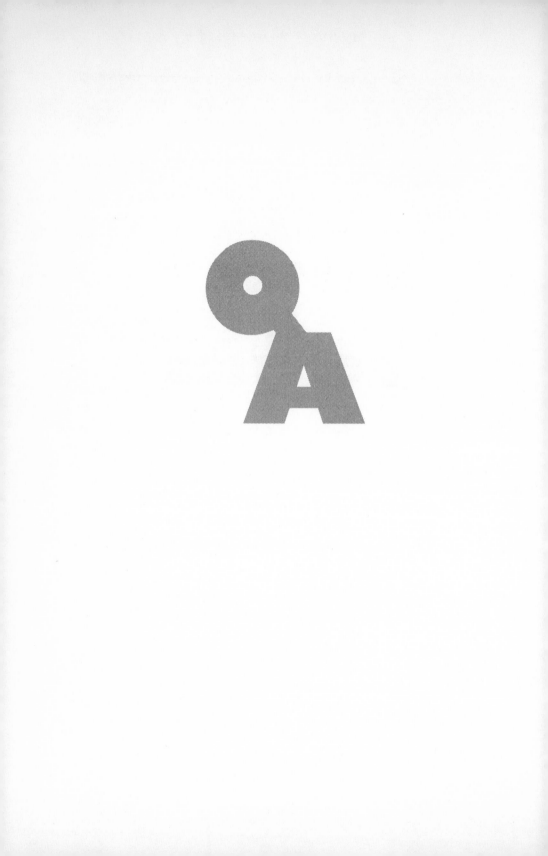

What does the French and Québécois symbol *fleur-de-lis* represent?

The English translation of *fleur-de-lis* is "flower of the lily." The Québécois and French symbol is a stylized depiction of a lily or a lotus flower and was adopted and used by French royalty to signify perfection, light, and life.

Legend has it that an angel presented Clovis I (circa 466–511 AD), the Merovingian king of the Franks, with a golden lily as a symbol of his purification when he converted to Christianity. Another legend claims that Clovis adopted the symbol after water lilies showed him shallow water where he was able to cross a river with his army and win a major battle.

Why is a small personal case for mementos called a "locket"?

Lockets are usually worn on chains around the neck and carry small personal items, photos, or memories of a loved one. They are the reason a small clipping or tress of hair is called a "lock of hair." The word *locket* probably arrived in England in 1066 with the invasion of William the Conqueror (circa 1028–1087), who would have used the Old French word *loquet* to describe a small lock or latch. The small ornamental case with a hinged cover and latch, as we know it today, surfaced in 1679.

Where did the expression "don't count your chickens before they hatch" originate?

"Don't count your chickens" is a commonly used saying similar to New York Yankees catcher Yogi Berra's warning that "it ain't over till it's over." First written in the sixth century BC, it is a quotation from one of Aesop's fables, called "The Milkmaid and Her Pail." It means "don't get ahead of yourself, because life is full of uncertainties." Aesop began life as a slave but was freed because of his wit and wisdom. "Don't count your chickens before they hatch" was first recorded in English in the late sixteenth century.

Why is a receding hairline said to reveal a "widow's peak"?

A widow's peak is hair that comes to a point at the top of the forehead. Today the term generally applies to men with receding hair, but it began as a reference to women with just such a pointed hairline. The reason it is called a widow's peak is because it resembles the pointed crest of a sixteenth-century mourning hood worn by widows when their husbands passed away. It was believed that if a woman developed a hairline resembling the front of that mourning hood, her husband would soon die. For a time, similar hair growth on a man was called a widower's peak and was equally bad news for the wife. The mourning hood was called a *biquoquet*.

What is the difference between the words *bickering* and *dickering*?

Even though they both involve a disagreement, there is a dramatic difference between *bickering* and *dickering*. *Bickering* now means to quarrel, but the word began as *bicken*, Dutch for "an attack involving a misunderstanding by slashing or stabbing." *Dickering* came from the Roman habit of packaging units of ten hides for bartering or haggling with barbarians. These packets were called *decuria* from *decem*, meaning "ten," and gave English the word *dicker*.

What is the origin of the word *maroon*?

Maroon is a dark reddish colour or a chestnut flavour. As a verb, the word means "to be put ashore on a deserted island" or "to abandon someone in isolation." However, the obscure use of *maroon* as a reference to slaves who escaped or were set free in the seventeenth century is lesser known. These runaway slaves lived in the mountains of the West Indies. At times they fought guerrilla wars against the Spanish, French, and British colonists. Jamaican maroons were among the first slaves to be proclaimed free by the British in 1715. Some were brought to Canada where they settled in Preston near Dartmouth, Nova Scotia, but the resettlement didn't go well, so most were relocated to Sierra Leone in West Africa, near where their ancestors had originally been captured.

    Maroon, as it is used in reference to runaway slaves, is a corruption of the Spanish word *cimmarón*, which means "wild, untamed." Over time it came to signify lost in the wilderness and gained its association with desert islands from stories such as the novel *Robinson Crusoe* by the English writer Daniel Defoe (1660–1731).

Why do people throw coins into a fountain?

There are thousands of fountains around the world inviting passersby to toss in coins for good luck, but they have all been inspired by the romance of the legend behind Rome's famous Trevi Fountain (Fontana di Trevi). Built over a thirty-year period in the mid-eighteenth century, the Trevi became the focus of a legend that said throwing a coin over one's shoulder and into the fountain meant one would visit Rome again. Pitching two coins ensured that the thrower would fall in love with someone from Rome, while tossing three coins signified the thrower would marry that someone.

Rome has 289 fountains. The Trevi Fountain was built from money raised by taxes on wine. It is located in Piazza di Trevi, which was erected to commemorate the completion of the Aqua Vergine in 19 BC.

What is a "Sphinx"?

Although the statue at Giza in Egypt is the most famous Sphinx, there is another. According to Greek mythology, the original Sphinx was a female winged creature with the body of a lion that attacked travellers near Thebes and then strangled and devoured those who couldn't answer her riddle: "What creature has one voice yet becomes four-footed, then two-footed, then three-footed?" Eventually, Oedipus defeated the Sphinx with the answer to the riddle: "A human crawls on all fours when a baby, walks on two feet when grown, and uses a staff when old."

In Egyptian mythology, the Sphinx is just as nasty but is wingless and male with the body of a lion. *Sphinx* is the Greek word for "strangler."

Why when we know the outcome do we say "it's all over but the shouting"?

If the outcome of a circumstance is known during a procedure is ended, we say "it's all over but the shouting." The expression comes from a widespread practice in early England. For centuries, when a straightforward public issue was to be decided, an assembly of townspeople was called for an informal election that was settled by shouting out a voice vote rather than by ballot. These assemblies were called "shoutings." When there was no doubt about the result even before the vocal vote was called, it was considered to be "all over but the shouting."

Why are unelected advisers to government leaders called a "kitchen cabinet"?

Most government leaders have unofficial non-elected advisers outside their legitimate cabinet and these people have been labelled a "kitchen cabinet." The expression was coined in 1832 when Andrew Jackson (1767–1845) was president of the United States. He used to hold frequent unofficial private meetings with three close friends, and in order to avoid scrutiny or criticism, they entered through the back door of the White House and then through the kitchen. From that time on the press referred to the president's inner circle as the "kitchen cabinet."

Why are heads of governments, cabinet chiefs, and church leaders called "ministers"?

The notion of the "prime" or first minister as the leader of government was introduced to Great Britain in 1646. Cabinet members or departmental ministers have been selected from elected representatives within that parliamentary system since 1625, but the reference to those holders of high office of the state as "minister" began in 1916. In this case, the word *minister* means "servant." They are servants to the crown, not their constituents. In the religious world, *minister* means a servant of the church hierarchy, not the congregation, and dates back to 1315.

Robert Walpole (1676–1745) is usually considered to be the first "prime minister" of Britain. However, he was not actually called that. In Britain the term did not become official until 1905.

When addressing a "prime" or "cabinet" minister, it is inappropriate to prefix the greeting with "mister" as in "Mister Prime Minister" or "Mister Minister," which is a common mistake in the American media and sometimes in Canada when used by uninformed reporters. The word *minister* is correct in itself, and adding *mister* is redundant. The U.S. prefix *mister*, as in "Mister President," is correct when greeting that country's president or his cabinet because they head a republic and not a crown state.

SPORTS

What is the "taxi squad" on a football team?

A "taxi squad" is made up of those professional football players who are under contract but not dressed for a game. They are four extra players beyond the roster limit who are only eligible to play on short notice as a substitute for an injured player if the team is shorthanded. The name "taxi squad" originated with the National Football League's Cleveland Browns, who at one time because the team couldn't put all its players on the forty-man roster found these extra players work as part-time taxi drivers.

What designates a colt, a filly, a mare, and a gelding in the world of Thoroughbred horses?

The official birth date of all Thoroughbred racehorses is January 1 of the year they were born regardless of the actual birth date. All horses are "foals" until they are a year old. Between the ages of two and five, males are called colts while female horses are fillies. Beyond the age of five, male horses are simply called horses while females are mares. A male horse that has been neutered is referred to as a gelding while one preserved for breeding purposes is a stallion. These designations are important because Thoroughbred racing uses age to determine equitable divisions for competition. *Gelding* is from the Viking word *geldr*, which means "barren."

Why is an athletic supporter called a "jock strap"?

It is difficult to imagine men competing in today's high-contact sports without that essential piece of equipment informally referred to as a "jock." Officially known as an athletic supporter, the device was introduced in 1874 to protect bicycle riders, who were called "bicycle jockeys," from hurting themselves on the crossbar after slipping off the pedals while navigating cobblestone streets.

Who was the first "cheerleader"?

Cheerleaders have become a major attraction at football and basketball games thanks to the enthusiasm of University of Minnesota student

Johnny Campbell, who stood during a football game in November 1898 and started leading the crowd in "rah, rah, rah" cheers. Since then the culture of cheerleading has often become larger than the game. Today cheerleaders don't just wave pompoms and lead cheers. They also perform difficult individual and synchronized gymnastic exercises.

Although the first cheerleader was a man, the vast majority since have been women.

President George W. Bush (1946–) was a college cheerleader.

ODDS & ODDITIES

The chance of hitting a hole-in-one in golf is 1 in 15,000.

The odds of becoming a professional athlete are 22,000 to 1.

The odds of catching a ball at a major-league baseball game are 563 to 1.

What is a "masse" pool shot?

A "masse" shot in pool is required when a ball is between the cue ball and the one a player is required to hit. To strike the target ball, a spin on the cue ball is necessary to curve around the obstruction. This procedure is accomplished by hitting the cue ball with the cue stick held nearly vertically and is known as a masse shot. The word *masse* derives from a description of a club used in medieval jousting tournaments.

Why do we call a person who show-jumps a horse an "equestrian"?

Equestrian is a word used to describe a competitive horseback rider and entered English in 1656 as meaning a "knight on horseback." The horse has evolved over fifty million years to become the majestic animal exhibited at various competitions today. *Equestrian* is from the Latin word for *horse*, which is *equus*.

QUICKIES

Did You Know ...

that the Detroit Tigers baseball team acquired its name in 1901 when the club's ball players wore yellow-and-black socks? Sports editor Philip Reid thought the socks were similar to those worn by the Princeton University Tigers football team.

that the New Jersey Nets basketball team chose its name because the word rhymed with the names of other professional sports teams in New York, namely the Mets baseball club and the Jets football team?

Why is a determined person said to be "hell bent for leather"?

It is a good idea to stay out of the way of anyone "hell bent for leather." The word *bent* has meant a mental inclination other than *straight* since 1586 and resurfaced as "bent out of shape," meaning "extremely upset or weird," during the 1960s. "Hell bent" means the disturbed subject is in a big hurry and extremely determined to achieve a goal. The "for leather" part derives from an 1889 reference to horseback riding, with the leather being the bridal and saddle. The expression then meant "riding very fast" and began as "hell for leather."

Hell is often used in association with speed, for example, "go like hell" or "run like hell."

WORK
&
MONEY

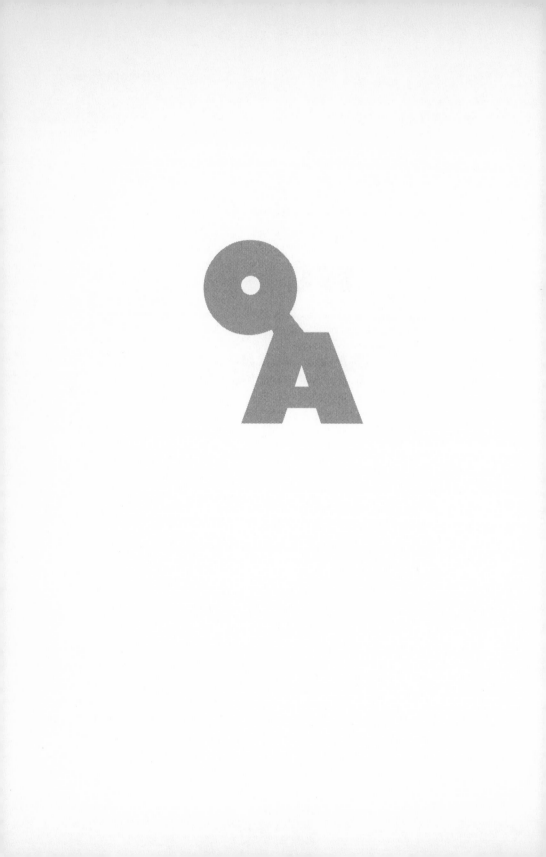

Why do we say that someone has "knocked off work" for the day?

To "knock off work" might be for any length of time, but it usually means for the day. The expression certainly had significance to those who first used it, because they were the oarsmen of a slave galley. To keep the ship on course, the slaves were kept rowing in unison by a drumbeat pounded out rhythmically on a block of wood. Different beats had different meanings, such as the left or right side only or altogether. These beats also signalled rest breaks and the end of a shift when the slaves were "knocked off" for the day.

Why is a serious response to a desperate situation called "fighting fire with fire"?

"Fighting fire with fire" means to meet a challenge with measures at least equal to the problem being confronted. The expression originates from a method still used to fight forest fires and serious grass fires. Settlers in the New World learned quickly to set fire to a strip of land in the wind path of an advancing prairie fire. By the time the wild fire reached the now-barren burned-off strip, it was stopped when it had nothing to feed on. This procedure is very dangerous when not practised by an expert. American writer Samuel Clemens (1835–1910), better known as Mark Twain, reported hearing the phrase during the 1850s.

Why is a useless project called a "boondoggle"?

The word *boondoggle* was first used in 1935 to describe "make-work" projects during the New Deal of American President Franklin Delano Roosevelt (1882–1945). It meant any useless task created simply to give men employment during the Great Depression. Surprisingly, the word comes from the Boy Scouts whose braided leather lanyard is simply cosmetic with no real purpose. It was named a "boondoggle" by R.H. Link after the leather frills worn by American frontiersman Daniel Boone (1734–1820). The word survives with the contemptuous political meaning of money wasted on unimportant or meaningless projects.

Why is buttering up a boss said to be "currying favour"?

If you are trying to get on someone's good side with insincere behaviour, your actions are "currying favour" from that person. *Curry* is a horse-grooming term for cleaning and rubbing down an animal. Within this expression, *favour* was originally Favel, the name of the half-man, half-horse centaur in the fourteenth-century satire *Le Roman de Fauvel*. Fauvel or Favel was very evil and cunning, and it was a good idea to get on the centaur's good side. You could do this by pampering or grooming or "currying Flavel."

How do the left and right sides of the brain influence a person's choice of career?

Most people tend to emphasize characteristics of the left side of the brain, which controls verbal and analytical skills such as speech, language, and grammar. Lawyers, accountants, politicians, business executives, salespeople, and teachers depend on these skills. On the other hand, the right brain is visual; it jumps easily to conclusions and it gets the big picture. Artists tend to exploit their right brains, while architects, engineers, and doctors effectively utilize both the left and right sides of their brains.

The fact that creative writers use language (governed by the left brain) for their artistic expression doesn't contradict that they are more influenced by the artistic right side. The American writer Mark Twain once sent a manuscript to his publisher with the following message: "Gentlemen: ....???"""333.......,,,,,,"(((((())))))!!!..;;;;:!" please scatter these through the attached according to your taste."

Why do men call a good friend their "buddy"?

Buddy is a masculine term for a close companion who can be counted on in a crisis. In wartime males become buddies during combat or while watching each other's back in a foxhole. The word originated with seventeenth-century Welsh and English coalminers who referred to a workmate with whom they shared the responsibilities of survival as a *butty*, which became *buddy* in North America.

Why is the head office called the "flagship" of a corporation?

We often use the word *flagship* to indicate the most important or largest component or unit within an industrial complex. This tendency derives from the navy where a flagship carried the admiral and flew his flag. The admiral's ship was the largest in the fleet, and just like today's CEO, the admiral required larger quarters and rooms to conduct strategy meetings.

What is the difference between a "job" and a "career"?

The noun *job* as "a piece of work" was first recorded in the mid-sixteenth century. By the mid-seventeenth century, the word had also come to mean "continuous labour for pay." The term began as *jobbe*, which is a variant of *gob* or *lump* and means specific work for money. *Career*, on the other hand, started out as the Latin noun *carrus*, or "chariot," and evolved into several meanings, including "to speed." Generally, during the Middle Ages, *career* was employed to describe a running course such as the sun's transit across the sky or even a race-course. In the sixteenth century, a track on a jousting field was called a career. In the early twentieth century, *career* began to mean the progression of "a life's work," while *job* remained a particular piece of work or a paid position of employment. *Career* can still mean a racecourse, only today it is run by rats.

Why is a "touchstone" the standard against which things are measured?

A "touchstone" is a figurative standard of value or quality against which something is measured. The word comes from ancient times when a special stone was used to guard against counterfeit money. The gold or silver content of coins wasn't well governed, so phony money was often mixed with other metals and passed off as authentic. Merchants tested the purity of coins by rubbing them on a hard black stone. The colour of the streak left on the "touchstone" disclosed the coins' true value.

Ultraviolet scanners provide a kind of touchstone for today's paper money. Passing a bill under the scanner gives an instant indication of its authenticity based on a number of security features built into the bill.

Who issued the first credit cards?

There once was a time when people only used cash. Credit was a personal issue between the dealer and individual customers. In the 1920s, gas companies and hotel chains started issuing cards for credit exclusively for use in their own establishments. By the late 1930s, some of these firms began recognizing one another's cards, but it wasn't until 1950 that the Diners Club came out with a fee-based card to use with a large number of unrelated businesses. Soon after, American Express took a similar approach. BankAmericard, which became Visa, issued the first bank credit card in 1959. MasterCard appeared in 1966.

Canadians own over fifty million Visas and MasterCards. Thirty percent of Canadian credit card holders don't pay their full bill each month.

Why are shares in a company called "stock"?

The modern concept of sharing capital ownership was initiated by the Dutch East India Company in 1612, which raised money by selling pieces of the business to the public. This process gave the Dutch East India Company the ability to grow and share its profits with its "shareholders." The original meaning of the word *stock* was the trunk of a tree. Like that trunk, "stock" to a corporation supplies the necessities of life to the branches. This nourishment to any size company is "cash."

Stocks and shares are the same thing. Stock refers to an overall ownership in one or more companies within a portfolio. Shares signify ownership of one specific individual company.

Today a "stock market" is a place where securities are bought and sold, but the first one in London, England, was a fourteenth-century fish-and-meat market and was so called because it had been built on a site formerly occupied by the "stocks" used for corporal punishment.

What is the "grey market"?

"Grey market" goods are legally sold through channels other than those authorized by the manufacturer. Unlike black market products, which may be counterfeits, grey market goods are the real thing. Entrepreneurs simply buy a product in one country where the item is significantly cheaper than another, then import it to the target market and legally sell the merchandise at a higher price. This situation commonly occurs with cigarettes and electronics, though importing legally restricted items leaves the "grey" and enters the "black" market. By avoiding the normal distribution fees or licences, consumers usually share in the profits of grey marketers through lower prices but are likely to discover that products acquired this way aren't supported or warranted by the manufacturer.

The existence of the grey market is an example of the economic practice called arbitrage. Grey market has a different meaning on securities markets where the term refers to the buying and selling of securities to be issued in the future and, therefore, not yet circulating.

PLACES

How did England get its name?

The country of England got its name from a Germanic tribe that migrated there in the fifth century AD. These Germans called themselves Anguls or Anglas, which became Angles around the fourteenth century. The Angle invaders called their new home Land of the Angles or Engla Land, which through time became England.

The German invaders called themselves Anguls because they were from a district in Schleswig that was shaped like a fishing hook. *Angul* was derived from the Latin *angulus*, meaning "corner," which originated in an earlier Indo-European word *ank*, or "to bend," which had given the district and the people that name.

The word *angling*, as in "fishing," also comes from the Latin *angulus* and was a reference to a "bent" fish hook.

How many cities are there with a population of a million or more?

The United Nations Population Division has projected that the world's population will become seven billion by 2013 and grow to 9.1 billion in 2050. Since most people continue to move to cities, the million-population club of urban centres grows ever more quickly. Rome, Italy, was the first city to reach a million in 133 BC, though after the fall of the Western Roman Empire, that city's population declined so precipitously that it wasn't until about 1930 that it again reached a million. London, England, achieved the million mark in 1810, and New York City attained it in 1875. In 2005 there were 336 cities in the world with populations exceeding one million.

What is the population of the world's largest cities?

Population of the world's cities is measured in two ways. One is by population within metropolitan boundaries. By that measure, Mumbai (formerly Bombay), India, is the world's largest city with almost twelve million people. Measuring by urban agglomeration, which means the city plus surrounding communities, Tokyo, Japan, leads with a staggering thirty-five million people, sixteen million more than Mexico City, the second-largest.

Measured as an agglomeration, Tokyo has a population of three million more inhabitants than all of Canada. Toronto, Canada's largest city, ranks about fiftieth in the world as an agglomeration of around 4.5 million people.

How did the city of Toronto get its name?

There are those who say that "Toronto" was a First Nations chief, while others insist the name refers to a Native tribe. Still others contend the name was derived from the Huron word *toronton*, meaning "meeting place." Research into early French explorers' maps from the 1670s, however, has uncovered the truth. These maps show present-day Lake Simcoe, seventy-five miles north of Toronto, as Lac Taronto. In Mohawk *taronto* means "fish trap." The French later applied the name to a trading post at the mouth of the Humber River, inside the boundaries of present-day Toronto.

Besides the trading post, the French also had Fort Rouillé built inside the area of today's Toronto. By the time the British captured the fort in 1760, it was generally known as Fort Toronto. In 1793 Lieutenant-Governor John Graves Simcoe changed Toronto's name to York because he didn't like aboriginal names. The name was changed back to Toronto in 1834.

The Simcoe counties of Tay and Tiny were named after Mrs. Simcoe's pet dogs.

How did the city of Calgary get its name?

In 1875, during trouble with the First Nations, the local North-West Mounted Police sent E troop under Inspector E.A. Brisebois to erect a barracks on the Bow River. When Brisebois wanted to name the new structure after himself, his commander, Lieutenant-Colonel James Macleod, overruled him and named the settlement Fort Calgary, after the ancestral estate of his cousins, the MacKenzies, in Scotland. The Gaelic translation of Calgary is "clear running water," . which certainly describes the Bow River.

The translation of the Blackfoot name for the area known as Calgary (briefly Fort Brisebois) was "elbow many houses." The translated Cree name for the area was "elbow house." Both Native references are to the Elbow River.

QUICKIES

Did You Know ...

that the eastern coast of Canada is closer to London, England, than it is to the country's own West Coast?

that in England the farthest one can get from the sea is sixty-five miles, while in Greece it is eighty-five miles?

that the summit of Mount Irazú in Costa Rica is the only place on Earth where one can see both the Atlantic Ocean and the Pacific Ocean?

that at sixty-four million square miles the Pacific Ocean is twice as large as the Atlantic Ocean and covers a greater area than all the land mass on Earth combined?

Why is a young rascal or rogue called a "scallywag"?

A "scallywag" is usually a reference to a mischievous, youthful little scamp who seems to cause trouble continually. The original English spelling of *scallywag* was *scalawag* and is a reference to Scalloway, one of the Shetland Islands, where the famous Shetland ponies are bred. The word was created as an insult to the residents of Scalloway whose horses were so much smaller than the standard breeds.

The hostile, damp, and chilly environment of the Shetlands is the major reason ponies bred there are so much smaller than standard horses. Their small stature helps them conserve body heat and huddle out of the wind behind low hills. Shetland ponies became extremely sought after in Britain during the nineteenth century when many thousands were used in coal mining to haul carts in the tunnels after a piece of legislation called the Mines Act banned children from working in the mines in 1847.

Scallywag is also used in the United States to describe Southerners who collaborated with Union Reconstructionists after the Civil War. The word has also been employed to describe unscrupulous politicians and men who won't work.

Why did Cape Canaveral become Cape Kennedy and then Cape Canaveral again?

Cape Canaveral, Florida, was named by the Spanish and began to appear on maps around 1564. After the 1963 assassination of President John F. Kennedy (1917–1963) and because he had been such a driving force behind the space program, Jacqueline Kennedy (1929–1994), his widow, asked President Lyndon Johnson (1908–1973) to rename the space facility located there after her late husband. Instead Johnson renamed not just the facility but the entire cape. The move was so strongly opposed by local residents that in 1973 the name Cape Canaveral was restored.

The space facility is still named the Kennedy Space Center. *Cañaveral* means "canebrake" or "canefield" in Spanish, and Cape Canaveral is usually interpreted as "Cape of Canes."

BELIEFS
&
SUPERSTITIONS

Why is the book of Christian scriptures called a "Bible"?

The Christian book of scriptures was first called the Bible by the Greeks. The ancient Phoenicians had found a way to make a form of paper from the papyrus plant, which gave us the word *paper*. They had done this in the city of Byblos, which is why the Greeks called the new paper *biblios*, and a collection of related writings or a book was soon called a *biblion*. By 400 AD, the word *Bible* emerged to exclusively describe the Christian collection of scriptures.

Byblos is now called Jubayl in modern Lebanon. The lowercase word *bible* now means any book of authority.

What does the H in "Jesus H. Christ" stand for?

The exclamation "Jesus H. Christ!" is often used as an attempt to avoid a blasphemous curse. Of course, even though it still takes the Christian Lord's name in vain, it is usually accepted as a joke. The epithet is based on "HIS" or "IHC," which is an abbreviation of Jesus's name in ancient Greek and is common in the earliest versions of the New Testament. It is still found on Catholic and Anglican vestments. The exclamation came from the misconception that these were Jesus's initials.

Why is someone living a "good" life said to be on the "straight and narrow"?

Someone on the "straight and narrow" is living a legal, moral, and disciplined life and was referred to in *The Pilgrim's Progress* by English writer John Bunyan (1628–1688). In that inspirational book, Pilgrim, the representative of everyman, must follow the "straight and narrow." The phrase has a biblical origin in Matthew 7:14: "Broad is the way that is the path of destruction but narrow is the gate and straight is the way that leadeth to the house of God."

Why is lighting "three on a match" considered bad luck?

Lighting three cigarettes in a row with one match was common practice among smokers until the advent of lighters and was especially practical to outdoorsmen or soldiers who needed to ration their matches. "Three on a match" became bad luck during the Boer War (1899–1902) when Commonwealth soldiers discovered the hard way that an enemy sniper would train his sights on a match when it was struck and then focus and fire by the time the third man lit his cigarette.

What is the origin of the expression "it's raining cats and dogs"?

The general legend about "raining cats and dogs" relates to the thatched roofs of the Middle Ages and would have you believe that when it rained, all sorts of creatures, including cats and dogs, slipped and fell in such abundance that it gave rise to the expression, but that's wrong! The truth is that the saying predates even the Dark Ages and goes back to a time when people believed that ghosts and goblins were around every corner. Cats and dogs had magical, mystical powers. Sailors believed that cats brought on storms and that witches rode those storms (with their cats). To the early Norsemen, dogs and wolves symbolized the wind, and the Viking storm god Odin was always shown surrounded by dogs. So during a violent rainstorm, an angry Odin's dogs were set loose, and the cats, symbolizing the rain, caused people to say, "It's raining cats and dogs."

The word *cat* is derived from the ancient Greek word *catadupe* and means "waterfall." In Latin *cata doxas* means "contrary to experience," or "an unusual fall of rain."

Why should heavy drinkers wear an amethyst?

An amethyst is a pale blue to dark purple crystallized quartz and is a precious stone found in modern-day Iran, Iraq, Brazil, India, and some parts of Europe. It was worn on the breastplates of high priests because the ancients believed that wearing or even touching an amethyst kept people from getting intoxicated no matter how much they drank. In Greek the word *amethyst* literally means "not intoxicating."

How many saints are there?

The first official canonization took place in 993 AD when Pope John XV (died 996 AD) declared Bishop Ulrich of Augsburg a saint. *Butler's Lives of the Saints*, published in 1759, had 1,486 entries. The revised edition in 1956 listed 2,565. Currently, an up-to-date version of the book is in the works, so the exact number of saints is unknown.

Pope John Paul II (1920–2005) canonized twelve people, which brought the total number of saints named during his pontification to more than 300, which is about half the number of saints named in the past 400 years.

During the first 800 to 900 years of Christianity, there was no formal recognition of sainthood. The number of martyrs and others of exceptional faith from that time are the main reason for the Feast of All Saints or All Saints Day held on November 1 and the vigil of which is called All Hollows Day or Halloween.

What is a "patron saint"?

Patron saints are chosen as guardians or protectors over specific areas of life. These can be chosen by people or groups without papal consent simply because the saint's interest or life experience relates to a group or individual. The church has, however, chosen many patron saints such as the writer Francis de Sales, who was picked to be the patron saint of writers and journalists. Angels can also be named as patron saints.

Who is Canada's patron saint?

Canada has two patron saints. Since French Catholics were the first Europeans to settle Canada, they brought their religion and customs with them, including the assignment of patron saints. St. Anne, the Virgin Mary's mother, shares patronage of Canada with Mary's husband, St. Joseph. St. Anne is also the patron saint of housewives, cabinet makers, and all women in labour. Her Roman Catholic feast day is July 26. St. Joseph shares his patronage of Canada with Mexico, China, Belgium, and carpenters. In 1870, Pope Pius IX (1792–1878) declared St. Joseph the universal patron of the church. St. Joseph's feast day is March 19.

What are "guardian angels"?

A "guardian angel" is a heavenly spirit assigned by God to watch over each person during his or her individual life. The angel is part of the dogma of the Roman Catholic faith and is there to help guide people and keep them from evil or danger. The feast to honour guardian angels is on October 2.

Like unidentified flying objects (UFOs), angels come in a variety of forms, depending on whose vision is believed. Moses was visited by an angel in the guise of a burning bush, while Jacob said that he saw wingless angels climbing a ladder to heaven. Witnesses swore they saw angels in human form beside the tomb of Jesus. Ezekiel (of the wheel fame) boasted that he saw cherubim with four wings, while Isaiah outdid him by claiming to witness seraphim angels with six wings. After that the common image of an angel with two wings, as depicted by most artists to this day, was settled on.

The English word *angel* is from the Greek *angelos*, meaning "messenger." The Hebrew word for angel is *malak*, which also means "messenger." In the Koran, angels are said to have two, three, or four pairs of wings or forelimbs, depending on how the Arabic word *ajnihah* is interpreted.

Who gets to be a "martyr"?

Martyrs are people who choose torture or death rather than renounce their beliefs or principles. The English word derives through Latin from the Greek *martur*, meaning "witness." The first Christian martyr is said to have been St. Stephen, who was stoned to death after being convicted of blasphemy by a Jewish court around 33 AD. Jewish martyrs include a group of forty who died during the Crusades when they refused to renounce their faith and accept Christianity. In Islam the first martyr is said to be an old female slave named Sumayyah bint Khabbab, who was tortured and killed in front of Mecca by polytheists, people who believed in many gods.

QUICKIES

Did You Know ...

that "bad-mouth" came to English through African American slaves and means to utter a curse or cast a spell on someone?

that the word *Zounds* is archaic British slang for "Christ's wounds"?

Why do Muslims pray five times a day?

Muslims pray five times a day in response to an order from God. Prayers must be said just before sunrise, after the sun peaks at noon, in the late afternoon, just after sunset, and between sunset and midnight. The ritual of prayer involves a series of actions that go with the words of a prayer. Everyday thoughts must be put aside before praying, otherwise no benefit will be realized. Everyone from the age of seven is encouraged to take part in prayer.

In the beginning, before life became too busy, Christians also prayed five times a day!

Why is not eating called "fasting"?

The original meaning of *fast* was "hold firmly," as in "she held fast to her principles." As a practice of not eating, fasting is all about maintaining firm self-control. Today fasting can take many forms and is practised by the religious and non-religious. As a protest, prisoners use it to demonstrate that their captors don't control their will or bodies. As a religious exercise, it is a demonstration of a person's steadfast allegiance to God. Some people fast simply to purge their bodies of its toxins.

The word *fast* began in Old English as *faest*, meaning "firmly steadfast" or "mentally strong," and has the same application to swiftness or running a long-distance race.

Why is an excessive enthusiast called a "zealot"?

A zealot is a supreme fanatic, often a bigot, and perhaps unfairly is best known in history as a radical Jewish political movement called the Zealots. This sect joined with several other Jewish groups to launch a rebellion in Palestine against the Roman Empire in the first century AD. Known for being aggressive, intolerant, and violent, the Zealots captured Jerusalem in 66 AD and held it for four years. When Rome finally recaptured the city, it was destroyed. The sect also captured the fortress of Masada and held it for several years against thousands of troops until the Romans set it on fire in 73 AD, leaving a handful of survivors to tell the tale.

The word *zealot* comes from the Greek *zēlōtēs*, which means "a fervent follower." It is a synonym of the Hebrew word *kanai*, which means "one who is jealous on behalf of God."

Why is an intolerant person called a "bigot"?

A bigot is someone who is intolerant of any religion, race, group, or politics other than his or her own. The word began as a curse and was first recorded in English in 1598 as meaning "a superstitious hypocrite." *Bigot* originated as *bi got* from a common Old French slur against the Normans that today would be translated as "By God!" with the intended meaning of "God damn it!"

Legend has it that when the first duke of Normandy, Rollo, was ordered to kiss the foot of the French king, Charles III (879–929), he refused by uttering the curse *"Bi got!"*

Why do we say that someone grieving is "pining"?

If a person is "pining away," he or she is tormented by longing or grief, because *pine*, in this case, has the same meaning as *pain*. In the early

English language, Christians referred to *pinian* as the consequence of the tortures and punishment of Hell. *Pinian* became both *pine* and *pain*. As time went on, *pine* acquired a softer meaning, more associated with Purgatory, that suggested languishing or wasting away, while *pain* retained its "hellish" origins. Today *pine* usually has a romantic context such as "pining" for a lost love.

Where do we get the expression "earn brownie points"?

The original "brownies" are little Scottish elves (wee brown men) who are believed to fix things and help out around farms when everyone is asleep. They were the inspiration for the name Lord Baden-Powell's sister, Agnes, gave to the branch of Scouts that serves younger girls from six through eight years of age. Brownie points are those accumulated by the girls for good deeds. Enough Brownie points earns a reward or significant badge of honour. The first modern use of "brownie points" was in 1951 when scoring them was offered as a strategy of good deeds for men to stay out of trouble with their wives.

FAUNA
&
FLORA

When and why do cats purr?

One of the great and endearing mysteries about cats is their use of purring to show affection, but they also purr when in danger or while giving birth or dying. Feral cats will even purr during a standoff with another cat. Cats only purr in the presence of humans or other cats. Because they are born blind and deaf, kittens depend on feeling the purring of their mothers to find comfort and a place to nurse. The kittens themselves start purring at one week. The purring of all adult cats derives from this mother-kitten experience, a form of communication often accompanied by kneading the paws as they did while nursing. Purring is by choice and is exclusive to domestic cats in that it occurs uninterrupted both during inhaling and exhaling. Big cats make a similar noise, but only while exhaling. Raccoons also produce a purring sound, but again only while exhaling. Cats choose to purr, but how is another question still a mystery to science.

Why is a species of whales called "sperm whales"?

The *sperm* in *sperm whale* is an 1830 abbreviation of *spermaceti*, which means "sperm of a whale." It was once believed that the waxy, gel-like substance in the snouts of these aquatic mammals was the seed of the male whale. Spermaceti was prized for its medicinal properties and was also used for candle oil. The material is, in fact, used by the whale to cushion its sensitive snout as it dives and has nothing to do with the animal's reproductive functions.

In 1471 the English alchemist Sir George Ripley (circa 1415–1490) suggested in "The Compound of Alchemy" that drinking a mixture of "whale sperm" with red wine would fight the chronic ills of growing old.

What does the "grey" mean in "greyhound"?

Greyhound dogs have been bred for hunting and racing and have extremely keen eyesight. They are one of the fastest land mammals and can reach speeds up to forty-five miles per hour. They were introduced to England from Celtic mainland Europe in the sixth century BC. The dogs come in a wide variety of colours, which indicates that the "grey" in their name has nothing to do with their hue. *Hound* is from the Old English word *hund*, and *grey* derives from the Old Norse *grig*, which was used generically for any fair or light-coloured dog. Greyhounds make wonderful pets and have been nicknamed Forty-Five-Mile-an-Hour Couch Potatoes.

All ancient variations of the word *grey*, as in *greyhound*, have the common meaning of "shine" or "bright."

Why do dogs circle so much before lying down?

Dogs turn around several times before lying down. They appear to be trying to make themselves comfortable, though it has been facetiously suggested that "they are looking for the head of the bed." The fact is that dogs have maintained this habit from their origins in the wild. Like their ancestors and cousins, such as wolves, coyotes, and foxes, domesticated dogs still turn circles to beat down a bed of tall grass.

Why do we say a "leopard can't change his spots"?

Much like "you can't teach an old dog new tricks," we sometimes say "a leopard can't change his spots" to underline that mature people can't alter who or what they are. Such a person's character is too indelible. The phrase about the leopard's spots comes from Jeremiah 13:23 in the Bible: "Can the Ethiopian change his skin or the leopard his spots?"

How did the beaver get its name?

A beaver is an industrious little rodent whose fur was the foundation of an industry that helped create Canada. At a time in history when knights wore armour, the hinged bottom portion of the helmet was called the "beaver," because when it was lifted for food or drink it revealed a man's beard, which is how the word became synonymous with body hair.

The helmet beaver derived its name from the Latin *bevere*, meaning "to drink." The furry little creature got its name from the Welsh word *befer*, meaning "bear."

How many natural wild "rabbits" are born each year in North America?

There are no rabbits native to North America and there never were. The North American animal is properly called a hare, so the answer to the above question is zero. Early North American settlers dropped the word *hare* from their vocabulary. The American term *jack rabbit* is an abbreviation of the original name *jackass-rabbit*, so named because of its long ears.

A "rabbit punch," describing an illegal action in boxing, comes from a gamekeeper's method of dispatching an injured rabbit by "chopping" it on the back of its neck with the side of the hand.

Why are some schemes called "hare-brained"?

The adjective *hare-brained* usually refers to a plan or action that is unexplainably preposterous. If there is any confusion about this word's meaning, it lies in the sixteenth-century dual spelling as both *hare-brained* and *hair-brained*. In any case, the word is a reference to the wildly odd mating season practices of hares, which are so bizarre that they are the origins of the expression "mad as a march hare."

Why are Siamese cats so fussy?

If you have ever wondered why Siamese cats are always "talking" or bossing you around, it may be because they are descendants of royalty.

Cats were revered in Siam where they were often selected to become receptacles of the souls of departed royals and senior government officials. When such a regal person died, a chosen cat would be taken to a temple where priests and monks would attend to their every need.

The first Siamese cats came to Europe and North America in the late nineteenth century from the Kingdom of Siam, which became Thailand in 1939. There are three popular lines of Siamese cats: seal points, chocolate points, and blue points.

QUICKIES

Did You Know ...

that even though the Jack Russell terrier's pedigree is still not recognized, the dog was named in 1907 after its breeder, Reverend John Russell (1795–1883), of Devonshire, England?

that cocker spaniels got their name from being bred to hunt peacocks?

that lions are the only cats to hunt in packs (prides)?

Why do we call a deliberately misleading story a "canard"?

A "canard" is a story or a statement that is a hoax or a lie. *Canard* is French for *duck*, but in English the word refers to a deliberate falsehood and is based on a French proverb about cheating or swindling. *Vendre un canard à moitié* literally translated means "to half sell a duck." However, the expression probably means "to sell half a duck." Selling a bag containing a half duck as if it were whole at a busy farmers' market would constitute a deliberate "lie" with the intention of cheating the purchaser.

The U.S. reason for invading Iraq has been called a canard.

What is the advantage of "sitting in the catbird seat"?

"Sitting in the catbird seat" means you have an advantage over the opposition. The catbird is a thrush, and like its cousin, the mockingbird, perches among the highest branches of a tree and has a warning cry that resembles that of a cat. "Sitting in the catbird seat" originated in the U.S. South in the nineteenth century and was regularly used on radio by Red Barber (1908–1992), the Brooklyn Dodgers' baseball announcer. Amused by the expression, Dodgers fan and humorist James Thurber (1894–1961) popularized the expression in a 1942 *New Yorker* story entitled "The Catbird Seat." As Thurber wrote, "'Sitting in the catbird seat' meant sitting pretty, like a batter with three balls and no strikes on him."

Why do we say someone is "happy as a clam"?

"Happy as a clam" seems to assume that the mollusk is indeed happy. This notion was probably inspired by the observation that if a clam is held sideways and looked at straight on it appears to be smiling. However, the expression is incomplete. It began as "happy as a clam at high tide." High tide is, of course, the time when clams can feed. High tide is also a time when clams are safe from clam diggers which, obviously, would make them very happy.

The word *clam* is derived from the same Scottish word that means "vise" or "clamp."

What makes a monarch butterfly unique?

The monarch is the only North American butterfly known to migrate. Scientists believed monarchs migrated for quite a long time, but it wasn't until 1975 that Cathy and Ken Brugger found the butterfly's wintering grounds in Mexico's Sierra Madre. There they discovered that the aboriginal peoples who lived in the area thought the butterflies represented spirits of dead children or the souls of lost warriors.

Logging and other kinds of human interference are threatening the survival of the Mexican monarch butterfly colonies. Climate change may be imperilling them, as well.

Why are wild horses called "mustangs"?

A mustang is a half-wild horse descended from the Arabian horses brought to the Americas by Spanish explorers in the sixteenth century. The word *mustang* comes from the Mexican-Spanish word *mestengo*,

QUICKIES

Did You Know ...

that the angle between the main vein and the smaller arteries of a leaf on a tree is exactly the same as the angle of the tree's trunk to its branches?

that broad-leaved deciduous trees (maple, beech, oak, et cetera) do not drop their leaves in the autumn because they die on their own? The trees cause their leaves to fall to save water during dry and cold spells.

that evergreen trees have adapted their leaves (needles) to minimize evaporation so that by gradually dropping them throughout the year they are able to keep them during the winter?

that the autumn splendour of dying leaves happens when sugar is converted into pigment? The more sugar trapped in the leaf, the more colourful the display, which is why the leaves of the sugar maple turn scarlet.

that evergreen and deciduous trees have been known to change, one into the other, when transplanted to a new climate?

meaning "stray animals that are ownerless." Today's mustangs are the offspring of generations of runaways and those horses stolen or recaptured by aboriginals. By 1800 there were millions of mustangs on the North American prairies, but as European settlers moved west, they killed and stole from the aboriginal stock until today, because they are still hunted, there are fewer than a thousand of these magnificent living symbols of independence still running free.

It is bitterly ironic that after four decades the Mustang car has more respect than its living namesake.

How did we get the expression "loaded for bear"?

"Loaded for bear" means you are well armed to meet any problem. In the days of muskets, the gunpowder charge could be adjusted depending on the size of the animals you expected to encounter in the wilderness. So if you were hunting bear, or simply entering their territory, you went into the bush well armed with an extra charge loaded into your musket. This expression originated in Canada.

Anyone familiar with Canadian wildlife knows that a simple walk in the bush can become a life-and-death confrontation with a dangerous animal. The bear is very territorial, viciously protective of its cubs, and extremely difficult to take down. Today "loaded for bear" means carrying a powerful rifle as well as a sidearm and a knife.

HOLIDAYS

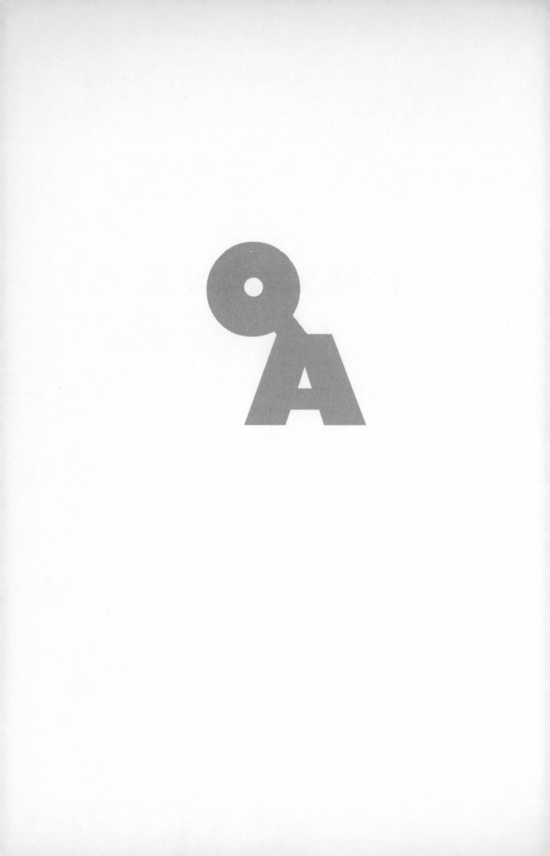

Why is a major celebration called a "jubilee"?

A jubilee is "a season of rejoicing" and comes from the ancient Hebrews. Fifty years after the Jews were freed from Egyptian bondage, they created a semi-centennial festival that lasted a full year within which all land would be left fallow and returned to its original owners. All debts were paid off and all slaves were emancipated. Declared a year of rest, the jubilee's arrival every fifty years was announced by the trumpeting of rams' horns throughout the land. A ram's horn in Hebrew is *yobhel*, which led to the English word *jubil* or *jubilee*.

Today there are silver jubilees (twenty-five years), golden jubilees (fifty years), diamond jubilees (sixty years), and platinum jubilees (seventy years). In 1897, Britain's Queen Victoria celebrated her diamond jubilee throughout the British Empire.

When is Mother-in-Law's Day?

According to a resolution passed by the U.S. House of Representatives in 1981, the fourth Sunday in October is set aside to honour mothers by marriage. Although the U.S. Senate hasn't adopted the resolution making the occasion official, the greeting-card industry continues to lobby for Mother-in-Law's Day and each year about 800,000 cards are sent to spouses' mothers.

When is Grandparent's Day?

In 1969 a sixty-five-year-old Atlanta man named Michael Goldgar returned home from visiting an aunt confined to a nursing home and realized that most of the elderly were treated as burdens by their children and grandchildren. He thought of earlier times when the elderly were a source of wisdom and the nucleus of a family. Goldgar began a seven-year campaign, including seventeen trips to Washington, D.C., at his own expense before President Jimmy Carter (1924–) signed legislation making Grandparent's Day the Sunday after Labour Day. As a result, more than four million cards are sent each year to grandparents.

Why is a calendar book of predictions and trivia called an "almanac"?

An almanac is an annual publication forecasting weather and providing other miscellaneous information relative to a calendar year. The earliest almanacs were largely preoccupied with astronomical and astrological information as well as dates for feasts and festivals. The seventeenth century saw almanacs begin to broaden their scope to include stories, poems, remedies, statistics, and jokes. Well-known almanacs include the *Farmer's Almanac*, which started publication in 1793, and *The World Almanac and Book of Facts. Poor Richard's Almanac*, produced by Benjamin Franklin (1706–1790) in the eighteenth century, is a fixture in English literature.

The word *almanac* came into English from Arabic through Spain in the fourteenth century as *al-manakh*, meaning "calendar."

How did pumpkin pie become associated with Thanksgiving?

There was no pumpkin pie at the first Thanksgiving, but because the plant's season coincides with the celebration and because it was Native Americans who taught the Pilgrims the pumpkin's value, the melon has become a traditional Thanksgiving dish. At first pumpkin was customarily served stewed as a custard or sweet pudding and was presented in a hollowed-out pumpkin shell. The first reference to pumpkin pie appeared in a book entitled *The History of New England* written by Edward Johnson in 1654.

AMERICANS
&
CANADIANS

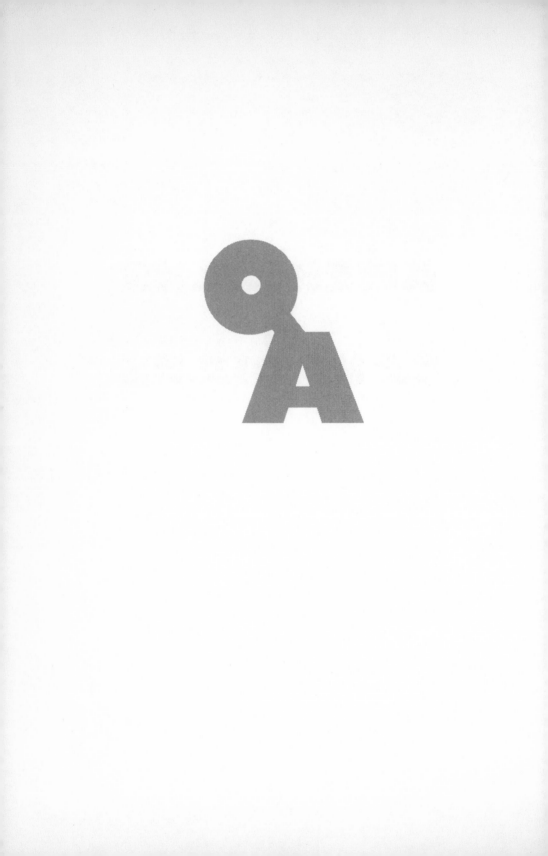

What is the full text of the Statue of Liberty poem?

The Statue of Liberty, formally called *Liberty Enlightening the World*, was a gift from the French to the people of the United States. It has stood since 1886 in New York City Harbour on Liberty Island. The famous poem engraved on a plaque at the base of the statue is a sonnet entitled "The New Colossus." It was written by Emma Lazarus (1849–1887) in 1883 to assist in raising money for the statue's pedestal. In 1903 the sonnet was engraved on a bronze plaque and put in place on a wall in the museum located in the statue's base. The poem was never engraved on the statue itself as frequently portrayed in editorial cartoons. Today the poem sings as a beacon not only to new immigrants but to all who seek to understand the human need for freedom and the *original* idea of the United States of America.

Emma Lazarus was a child of very successful Jewish immigrants who extended her universal compassion beyond her own cultural heritage. The full text of "The New Colossus" is as follows:

> Not like the brazen giant of Greek fame,
> With conquering limbs astride from land to land;
> Here at our sea-washed, sunset gates shall stand
> A mighty woman with a torch, whose flame
> Is the imprisoned lightning, and her name
> Mother of Exiles. From her beacon-hand
> Glows world-wide welcome; her mild eyes command
> The air-bridged harbor that twin cities frame.
> "Keep ancient lands, your storied pomp!" cries she
> With silent lips. "Give me your tired, your poor,
> Your huddled masses yearning to breathe free,
> The wretched refuse of your teeming shore.
> Send these, the homeless, tempest-tost to me,
> I lift my lamp beside the golden door!"

What Canadian resource do Americans need more — oil or water?

The Alberta tar sands have attracted the interest of the United States, and though Canada already accounts for 16 percent of U.S. oil consumption, new technology may someday diminish the Americans' need for carbon-based fossil fuels. Water is another matter. Each day 4,755 billion gallons of water are funnelled through water pipes, turbines, and irrigation systems in the United States. This massive activity represents about twelve times the average daily flow of the Mississippi River. The average per person need in the United States is 2,700 gallons, or 370 billion gallons in total each and every day. With American thirst for water increasing by 19 percent per year, Canada's water will become more than a mirage, it will be a necessity.

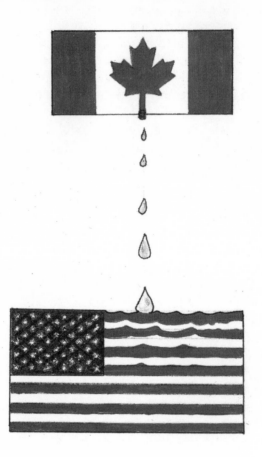

What colour is the Canadian flag — white or red?

The Canadian flag is red. On February 15, 1965, when Canada's new flag became official and flew over the country for the first time, the ceremonious proclamation read: "A red flag of proportions two by length and one by width containing in its centre a white square the width of the flag with a single red maple leaf therein."

When did the United States draw up modern-day plans for the invasion of Canada?

In 1974 it became public that in 1930 the United States had drawn up a strategic plan that included a successful invasion of Canada. The scheme was called "Plan — Red." It involved attacks on Montreal and Quebec, Winnipeg's railway centre, Ontario's nickel mines and power generation, and the Great Lakes. Naval blockades were to be set up on the Atlantic and Pacific coasts, and Halifax was to be captured and occupied. This proposal was one of several contingencies that could be used if the United States went to war with Britain, Japan, Germany, or Mexico.

The "Red" in the plan's title actually refers to Britain (Canada, as part of the British Commonwealth, was usually scarlet on maps) and was part of a global strategy for war with that nation. Plots for war with Japan were coded "Orange," war with Germany was "Black," and Mexico was "Green." A "White" plan was drawn up for a domestic insurrection, and a "Purple" proposal existed for war with a Central American country.

The idea that war was possible with Britain may have stemmed from a treaty between Britain and Japan that ended in 1924. The treaty prompted the United States to come up with a "Red-Orange" strategy that considered the threat of a British-Japanese alliance.

Of course, contingency plans are necessary, and as history from the time of World War I and World War II records, the Americans were very reluctant to go to war with anyone.

When did Canada plan to invade the United States?

It seems more than mildly absurd, but during the 1920s, while serving as the director of Canadian Military Operations and Intelligence, a man named James Sutherland Brown drew up "Defense Scheme Number One." He had heard that the Americans had drafted a similar plan for Canada's invasion, and as a descendant of United Empire Loyalists and because the United States had made several sorties into Canada during the nineteenth century, he didn't trust his southern neighbours. The proposal would have mobilized Canadian forces to capture and establish bases in Seattle and Minneapolis, stalling the U.S. Army long enough for the British to come to Canada's rescue. Considering modern-day circumstances, including the American interest in the Arctic and other Canadian resources, maybe Brown was ahead of his time.

BASEBALL

Why is the position between second base and third base called shortstop?

Baseball began with four outfielders and only three infielders to guard the bases. In 1849, D.L. Adams (1814–1899) realized that three men could cover fly balls in the outfield and that by moving one of these outfield players to the infield he could keep a lot of ground balls from getting through by "stopping them short," thus giving the new position its name of shortstop. Technically, this position is still an outfielder.

Why is an easily caught pop fly in baseball called a "can of corn"?

The legend is that in the days before supermarkets, small grocery store owners placed their tins of canned corn on the top shelves because they stored well and didn't sell as quickly as fresh corn. For most customers this system put the cans out of reach. The store owner or clerk needed a broomstick to reach up and topple the can of corn from the shelf and easily catch it by hand or in an apron.

Why are the pitcher and catcher collectively called "the battery"?

A *battery* is a military term for artillery and its use in baseball to describe a pitcher and a catcher alludes to the fact that the battery is the principle attack force for the small army of nine players on a baseball diamond. There is also an earlier theory that the baseball term derives from telegraphy where the word *battery* (also borrowed from artillery) defines the sender (pitcher) and the receiver (catcher).

How did the World Series get its name?

There is a myth that the World Series was named after the *New York World* newspaper, which was established in 1860 and was sold in 1930 after merging with the *Evening Telegram*, becoming the *New York World Telegram*. However, the *World* had nothing to do with naming baseball's annual classic.

In 1884 a series of games between the National League and American Association champions was reported by the press as contest to decide baseball's "World Champions." When the modern series began in 1903, the reference evolved (within all newspapers) into the "World Series" simply to hype the contest.

Who introduced the first catcher's mask?

The first baseball catcher's mask was a fencer's mask introduced by Harvard University's Fred Thayer in 1877. It wasn't until 1890 that the major leagues adopted the idea that all catchers should wear protective masks.

Who invented baseball's hand signals?

In 1869 the Cincinnati Red Stockings began utilizing a system of hand signals based on military flag signals that soldiers had used while playing baseball during the Civil War. Baseball's hand signals evolved from the earliest days of the game. Consequently, there are many moments and persons involved in their development, but none more important than a five-foot-four-inch, 148-pound centre fielder named William "Dummy" Hoy (1862–1961).

Hoy was the first deaf baseball player to make the major leagues. One afternoon in 1889, as a centre fielder with the Washington Senators, Hoy set a major-league record by throwing out three base runners at home plate. His is a fascinating story, but although not recognized in baseball's Hall of Fame, Hoy and his coaches and teammates developed an advanced system of hand gestures to overcome Hoy's deafness, which was a key impetus in the hand-signals evolution. Even umpires started physically indicating the batting count to communicate with Hoy. He couldn't hear the crowd, but Hoy's legacy is a major part of each and every ball game played to this day.

William Hoy played fourteen years in the majors, retiring in 1902 with a .288 lifetime batting average, 2,054 hits, and 726 runs batted in. His 597 career stolen bases still rank seventeenth in history.

During a regular nine-inning baseball game, more than 1,000 silent instructions are given — from catcher to pitcher, coach to batter or fielder, fielder to fielder, and umpire to umpire.

What is a "corked bat"?

Some baseball players, like Sammy Sosa, believe that the spring from a "corked bat" adds distance to a struck ball. Even though physicists say this notion is nonsense, occasionally someone will try to use one. The basic method of corking a bat is to drill a straight hole into the top about one inch wide and ten inches deep. Then, after filling the cavity with cork, the player plugs the hole with a piece of wood and sands it smooth. A corked bat is illegal only if used in play.

SCIENCE & TECHNOLOGY

How were microwave ovens discovered?

Masters of the culinary arts may have disdain for the microwave oven, but for most modern kitchens they are essential. The cooking use for microwaves was discovered by accident in 1945 when an American scientist named Percy Spencer (1894–1970) noticed that a candy bar in his pocket had melted while he was testing a magnetron, a tube that generates microwaves for use in radar systems. After experimenting with popcorn and a famous boiled egg, Spencer proved that microwaves could cook things.

Percy Spencer worked for the Raytheon Company, and it was that firm that manufactured the first microwave ovens in 1947. They were mainly sold to restaurants because they were the size of small refrigerators and were too expensive for the general public.

What was the initial purpose of the chainsaw?

In unskilled hands, a chainsaw can be dangerous. It might even cut through an arm or a leg. Ironically, that was what the first chainsaw was invented for. A German named Bernard Heine (1800–1846) invented the chainsaw in 1830. It was called an osteotome. In those days before general anesthetics, surgeons depended on speed to shorten the suffering of patients. The chainsaw was designed to speed up amputations by cutting through bone more quickly than was possible with conventional methods. The device was operated by turning a crank manually, much like you would if you were using a hand mixer. A Swiss German, Andreas Stihl (1896–1973), patented and developed an electric chainsaw for cutting wood in 1926. Three years later he patented a gas-powered model. Stihl is generally regarded as the father of the modern chainsaw.

How did the toilet get its name?

Toilet seems an odd name for the bathroom's chief plumbing fixture, but it makes sense when you consider that since the seventeenth century, "toilette" meant a lady's dressing room. The chief purpose of the room was for cleaning up or changing clothes. The other business was done in an "outhouse." When a lavatory became attached during the early nineteenth century, the room changed its main purpose and not only kept its name toilette but applied it to the regal new sitting

QUICKIES

Did You Know ...

that Bic pens were invented by Hungarian Lazlo Biro but were named after the French Baron Biche who manufactured and marketed them?

that the word *blog* is an abbreviation of *weblog*, an Internet site or "log" of items of interest to its author?

that *phishing* is the act of getting personal details surreptitiously through fake emails or websites and is simply a variation of the word *fishing*?

device. The beauty care and implements or "toiletries" assembled there were so named because they were placed on a fabric table cover called a toile. A toile, like a doily, is a netted decorative cloth.

Why is aluminum also spelled aluminium?

Aluminum is the most abundant metal in the Earth's crust where it is principally found in combination with bauxite. In 1808 when the English scientist Sir Humphry Davy (1778–1829) was figuring out how to isolate aluminum, he first called it alumium. In 1812, though, he renamed the metal aluminum, which is how it is still known in North America. That same year, however, the British decided the metal should be called aluminium to conform to the ending of most other related elements that end in *ium* such as sodium, potassium, et cetera. In 1812, Britain's *Quarterly Review* stated: "Aluminium, for so we shall take the liberty of writing the word, in preference to aluminum, which has a less classical sound."

What caused synthetic fibres to replace silk?

Silk is a fine, lustrous, natural fibre made from secretions by very small silkworms to produce cocoons. The cultivation of silk began more than

5,000 years ago in China, and the process is very manual and expensive. In 1935, while China and Japan were at war and the silk supply to Western countries was interrupted, scientists at the chemical giant DuPont came up with the synthetic fibre nylon as a replacement. The first commercial nylon products were toothbrush bristles in 1938 and women's stockings in 1940. Uses for the material expanded dramatically during World War II when it was substituted for silk in parachutes and replaced organic fibres in ropes, tents, ponchos, and many other products.

The synthetic textile fibres Orlon and Dacron were introduced by DuPont in 1948 and 1951 respectively. The registered proprietary names of DuPont's synthetic fibres begin with a random generic symbol such as *nyl* as in nylon and end in *on* from cotton.

It took three years to come up with the name *nylon*. An early front-runner was "no-run," which was abandoned because it wasn't true. Some people think that the word *nylon* is a combination of the abbreviation for New York City, NY, and the first three letters in London, but DuPont denies that.

Why is a manual counting board called an "abacus"?

The abacus is an ancient counting device with movable counters strung on rods and is used to solve arithmetic problems. Computers and calculators have made the apparatus obsolete. The word *abacus* has Semitic roots and came to English through the Greek word *abax*, meaning "dust" or "sand." Before the board with the beads, the ancients sprinkled a flat surface with fine sand for drawing geometric diagrams and solving mathematical problems. In 1387, written Middle English began referring to the sand-board calculator used by the Arabs by its Latin form *abacus*.

Who coined the expression "garbage in, garbage out"?

"Garbage in, garbage out" became famous when used by the brilliant lawyer Johnnie Cochran (1937–2005) during the O.J. Simpson trial. Its source is the computerese-abbreviated GIGO, which surfaced during the early 1960s. The acronym means that computers can only give you what has been put into them. Unfortunately, in spite of this shortcoming, some people insist on believing computers can't be wrong, so we get the expression "garbage in, Gospel out."

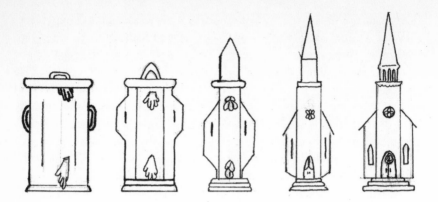

Why is an alias or electronic nickname called a "handle"?

An alias intended to conceal a user's real name or identity within an electronic message is called a "handle." Consider that *handle* is an extension of the word *hand* and is used to describe something you can get you hands on. Clearly, though an alias can be used to avoid revealing personal data, a figurative "handle" offers a way of getting hold of someone without disturbing that anonymity. The term was popular with ham radio operators and resurfaced during the CB radio craze of the 1970s and is now used on the Internet.

In the jargon of the 1870s, titles such as "sir" or "madame" were introduced to common English as "handles."

Shortwave radio operators are called "hams" from the call letters of an amateur wireless station set up by three members of the Harvard Radio Club whose last names began with the letters *H*, *A*, and *M*.

Why are the instruments used for sending and receiving sound called "radios"?

The device we call a radio took its name from radio telegraphy and was commonly referred to as the wireless up until World War II when the military preference for radio caused that name to catch on to describe the revolutionary receptacle of sound. The word *radio* is derived from *radius*, Latin for "spoke of a wheel" or "ray of light," because transmitted sounds travel out in all directions from a centre hub like the spokes of a wheel.

ODDS & ODDITIES

The chance that Earth will experience a catastrophic collision with an asteroid in the next 100 years is 1 in 5,000.

The odds of a meteor landing on one's house are 182,138,880,000,000 to 1.

The term *radio* was first used to describe the sound-broadcasting medium as an industry in 1922.

How much space junk is orbiting Earth?

The U.S. Air Force estimates that 9,000 pieces of space junk larger than ten centimetres across are currently orbiting the Earth with thousands of more smaller pieces. Space junk has only scored one confirmed hit on an active spacecraft. In 1996 a French military satellite was hit and knocked into a new orbit. The international space station has been forced to take evasive action on three occasions. *Vanguard 1*, a U.S. satellite launched in 1958, is the oldest piece of space junk still up there.

Why is a black hole black?

Black holes in space seem to be a recent phenomenon, yet Albert Einstein (1879–1955) predicted them in his theory of relativity in 1915. They are the incredibly dense centres of dead stars. Black holes appear black because their gravitational fields are so huge that even light can't escape. We find and measure black holes by calculating the orbits and other behaviours of nearby stars or gas clouds. Black holes capture our imagination because we believe that should we fly a spacecraft anywhere near them they will capture us. The Hubble Space Telescope has taken pictures of many suspected black holes. One is the core of Galaxy NGC 4261.

Why can't you escape a black hole?

There is no known escape from a black hole. To escape Earth, we have to travel at 25,000 miles per hour. If we go any slower, we won't break the planet's gravitational pull. When we run out of fuel, we will fall back to the ground. Black holes are even harder to escape. To get out of a black hole, you must go faster than the speed of light, and Albert Einstein's theory of relativity says that is impossible.

SELECTED EMAILS FROM READERS

Question: I am a recreational therapist (I do activities for seniors). One of the activities we do is trivia, and from time to time I use your books and the seniors find it very interesting. Tonight I used *Now You Know More*, and one of my residents had a question that I wondered if you could help us with. I looked in all your books and I couldn't find it. The question is: Why is a key that opens all locks called a "skeleton key"?

— Michelle Garvie, Montreal, Quebec

Answer: A "master key" is designed to open a specific set of several locks. Although these locks have individual keys, they also have a second tumbler system within the mechanism that enables the master key to open any one within that set. A "skeleton key" is a key ground down by criminals to pick a lock by avoiding the wards in a warded lock. Warded locks are those opened with a long-stem cylindrical shaft with a single flat rectangular tooth and are mostly out of fashion. They were called skeleton keys because they had been filed down to the "bare bones."

An underworld slang term for a skeleton key is *screw*, which is why convicts call guards in a prison "screws" — because they carry the keys.

Question: When oil is taken out of the ground, do they fill in the hole with anything? If they don't, wouldn't that cause the earth to eventually cave in?
— Larry Wilcox, St. Thomas, Ontario

Answer: Deep underwater, and deeper underground, scientists see surprising hints that gas and oil deposits can be replenished, filling up again, sometimes rapidly. This process is called "resting."

Question: I have a question I cannot seem to find the answer for. The question is: How do they select the people to be on a list of possible jurors? Any insight into this would be most helpful, especially at our coffee shop.
— Kathrine and Barbara Cowan, Wallaceburg, Ontario

Answer: In Ontario, to serve as a juror, you must be at least nineteen years old and a Canadian citizen. The provincial government chooses names randomly from the municipal voters' list to comprise a jury panel to be called into court. Final jury members are selected by drawing fifteen to twenty names of those called from a box in the courtroom by a court clerk. At this time if you wish not to serve you must appeal to the judge. You are disqualified for jury duty if you are an officer, lawyer, or an employee of the Ministry of the Attorney General (or certain other occupations), or you have been convicted of certain criminal offences within the past five years. Your participation is a legal obligation.

Question: I received *Now You Know Almost Everything* for Christmas and quite enjoyed it. I haven't had the opportunity to look at Volumes 1 and 2 of your books, so if the answers to my four questions are in them please direct me there. I was speaking to a cousin in England about staying in a hotel in London this summer, and he said, "This will cost you a pretty penny." My son recently started working in the construction industry and wondered why buildings had "stories." A visit to a local restaurant made us wonder why a

Coke was a "soft drink." And why are people who have retired "living the charmed life"?
— Robb Watts, Saskatoon, Saskatchewan

Answer: The reason levels in buildings are called "stories" is fascinating and is included in *Now You Know More*, the second volume of my series. The word *pretty* has several meanings besides "pleasant to look at." It can also mean "considerable," so just as "pretty please" means "a lot of begging," a "pretty penny" means a "great number of pennies." Colas and other carbonated beverages are called "soft drinks," as opposed to "hard drinks," because a soft drink comes from "soft water" and can be traced back to water found in natural springs first marketed as soft drinks in Paris during the seventeenth century. Back then the beverage was water and lemon juice sweetened with honey. William Shakespeare originated the expression "charmed life" in *Macbeth* when Macbeth tells Macduff near the end of the play as the two fight:

> Thou losest labour.
> As easy mayst thou the intrenchant air
> With thy keen sword impress as make me bleed.
> Let fall thy blade on vulnerable crests,
> I bear a charmed life, which must not yield
> To one of woman born.

QUESTION & FEATURE LIST

QUESTION AND FEATURE LIST

People

Sailing & the Sea

Sports

Work & Money

Places

Beliefs & Superstitions

YOUR QUESTIONS

If you have a question and haven't found the answer in my first four volumes of *Now You Know: The Book of Answers*, I would like to find the answer for you. Please send your questions to me by regular mail to:

Now You Know c/o Dundurn Press, 3 Church Street, Suite 500, Toronto, Ontario, Canada, M5E 1M2 or via email directly to dlennoxc593@rogers.com

We will credit your name and hometown if your question is used in a future volume.